A Selection from the Russell Sage Foundation

A Selection from the Russell Sage Foundation

Ann Greer
Consulting Editor

BROWN REPRINTS
Dubuque, Iowa

INTRODUCTION TO THE
REPRINT OF

Eugene Smith's

CRIMINAL LAW IN THE
UNITED STATES

by

Gilbert Geis

This book owes its origin to the fact that in 1910, for the first time in its 38-year-old history, the International Penal and Penitentiary Congress was convened in the United States. In anticipation of the Washington meeting, scheduled for the handsome Pan-American Building which had just been given by Andrew Carnegie to the Bureau of American Republics, the Russell Sage Foundation and the American Prison Association commissioned the writing of five volumes to report on the state of crime, criminal law, and the treatment of offenders in the United States. The five-volume set was to be distributed to Congress delegates as souvenirs of their participation in the Washington meetings. Eugene Smith was an obvious choice to prepare *Criminal Law in the United States*. A lawyer, he had been secretary, then president of the Prison Association of New York over the past twenty-five years. More importantly, he had written extensively and fervently in support of the indeterminate sentence, the most controversial topic on the Congress agenda, and an issue that pitted the United States delegation against most of the European representatives. The strength of Smith's advocacy of indeterminancy in sentencing could be read from, among other things, an article he wrote for *The Independent* in 1905, which concluded: "In the universal adoption of the indeterminate sentence, with all that it logically involves, rests the strongest hope for final victory in the contest, which has heretofore been a losing contest, for the suppression of crime."

Historians tend to trace the origin of the idea of the indeterminate sentence back to Benjamin Rush (1745-1813), a physician who was one of the signers of the Declaration of Independence. Rush advocated a "court" that would visit jails and prisons several times a year and, after reviewing evidence on the offender's adjustment, would then determine the nature and the duration of the punishment that he would have to undergo. The first major implementation of the principle of indeterminate sentencing appeared under Alexander Maconochie (1787-1860), a British naval officer who in 1840 was placed in charge of the penal colony on Norfolk Island in New South Wales. Maconochie, described by his biographer as "a deeply religious man, of generous and compassionate temperament, and convinced of the dignity of man," did away with traditional delimited prison sentences and introduced release by means of good behavior and industry. Maconochie's justification for his program reads very much as the panegyrics presented seventy years later by Eugene Smith for the edification of delegates to the Washington session of the International Penal and Penitentiary Congress:

> I think that time sentences are the root of very nearly all the demoralization which exists in prisons. A man under a time sentence thinks only how he is to cheat that time, and while it away; he evades labor, because he has no interest in it whatever, and he has no desire to please the officers under whom he is placed, because they cannot serve him essentially; they cannot in any way promote his liberation. . . .

Under Maconochie's system, each convict, rather than being sentenced to a term of years, was charged with a certain number of "marks," based on the seriousness of his offense. Before he could be released, he had to redeem these marks by good conduct, labor, and study; and the more rapidly this was done, the quicker his release. As Maconochie put it: "When a man keeps the key to his own prison, he is soon persuaded to fit it to the lock."

The system developed by Maconochie received its most prominent subsequent expression in the 1850s in the so-called Irish system of prison administration. The Irish system was said to operate as a "filterer between the prison and the public, by which the reformed convicts will be separate from the unreformed, the former to be advanced toward personal liberty and restoration to society, the latter to be returned for further penal treatment." Indeterminancy was combined with a *ticket of leave*, or parole, system, which permitted conditional release of convicts judged suitable for work in the community. The program was said to be something of a penological wonder; of 559 prisoners released in Ireland, one study reported, only 17 had had their tickets of leave revoked.

In 1865, Gaylord Hubbell, a former warden of the New York state prison at Ossining, visited Ireland and, as Philip Klein notes in *Prison Methods in New York State*, Hubbell returned with "a glowing report" on the Irish system. Thereafter, a vast literature on the subject began to develop. From 1865 to 1870, Klein observes, using a metaphor that now, when the indeterminate sentence is under severe attack, seems unconsciously close to the truth, the idea spread "like an avalanche." In 1870, Enoch Cobb Wines (1806-1879), a former schoolteacher and minister, who was then secretary of the Prison Association of New York (the same position that Eugene Smith held for twenty years), established the National Prison Association, and convened its first meeting in Cincinnati. There the group adopted a Declaration of Principles that today—more than a century later—continues to be regarded as the Pentateuch of criminal corrections. Blake McKelvey in *American Prisons* has admirably caught the spirit that took over at those Cincinnati meetings in 1870:

The convention was in the hands of reformers who had arrived with prepared speeches while the traditions had no spokesmen. Overwhelmed with inspired addresses, with prayer and song and much exhortation, even the hard-headed wardens were carried up for a mountain-top experience. In their enthusiasm for the ideal they rose above the monotony of four gray walls, men in stripes shuffling in lock step, sullen faces staring through the bars, coarse mush and coffee made of bread crusts, armed sentries stalking the walls. They forgot it all and voted for their remarkable declaration of principles. Among the principles were the following:

—Reformation, not vindictive suffering, should be the purpose of penal treatment of prisoners.
—Classification should be made on the basis of a mark system, patterned after the Irish system.
—Rewards should be provided for good conduct.
—The prisoner should be made to realize that his destiny is in his own hands.
—The aim of the prison should be such as to gain the will of the prisoner and conserve his self respect.
—Society at large should be made to realize its responsibility for crime conditions.

Also included was support of the idea of the indeterminate sentence:
—Indeterminate sentences should be substituted for fixed sentences, and the gross disparities and inequities in prison sentences should be removed.

The indeterminate sentence philosophy became partially translated into practice in 1877 at the reformatory in Elmira, New York, a new type of institution for young first offenders under the direction of Zebulon R. Brockway (1827-1920), often regarded as the greatest prison warden America has produced. Elmira received what now would be called "a good press." As Negley K. Teeters, a preeminent historian of correctional matters, notes: "Many states followed the example of New York in building reformatories and blowing reports from the superintendents filled the penal journals for many years." Teeters adds, however: "There was so much enthusiasm for the new idea that its advocates did not realize that it was only another form of repressive institutionalization, with much regimentation."

It can be noted, therefore, as part of the background against which the present book was written, that in 1910 the United States found itself deeply committed to advocacy of the indeterminate sentence. There was, for one thing, widespread dissatisfaction with traditional practices which, as Eugene Smith observes, were showing comparatively high recidivism rates. For another thing, prison practices in the United States were being given a large measure of their articulation by men of extremely high principles (often related to equivalent kinds of incomes), whose views of their fellows tended to be derived more from tracts on moral philosophy than from dealing with human beings. Lastly, the United States had developed a vested interest in the indeterminate sentence and its success. Already credited with development of the penitentiary, the juvenile court, and the system of probation, this country saw itself as a pioneer in the treatment of criminal offenders, and a nation with a good deal to offer what were regarded as the more tradition-bound and conservative countries of the world.

Shortly after he had founded the National Prison Association, Dr. Wines, that man of "sustained and even relentless energy," was instrumental in establishing the International Penal and Penitentiary Congress, envisioning it as a "sounding board" for new ideas, particularly as such new ideas emerged in different parts of the world.

The Congress first met in London in 1872. At its third gathering, in Rome in 1885, the delegates expressed themselves in favor of determinate sentences. "The maximum punishment for each offense should be fixed by law, the judge having no power to exceed it." This pronouncement was expressed in even sharper terms at the Sixth Congress in Brussels in 1900. "As to penalties," the delegates resolved, "the system of indeterminate sentences is inadmissible."

The United States delegation, feeling rather nonplussed, took this result with something less than total good grace, foreshadowing the reappearance of the issue on the Washington agenda. In his report on the Brussels meeting, Samuel Barrows, leader of the American group, wrote:

> Perhaps no advocate of the indeterminate sentence supposed that it would receive unqualified acceptance. . . . The traditional theory of a definite penalty is so strongly intrenched in statute and practice that to dislodge it is something like the task of removing Gibraltar. The indefinite sentence will not find full scope and acceptance until every vestige of the idea of retaliation or social vengeance disappears from our criminal codes and judicial administration.

Indeterminacy was not on the Congress' agenda when the group met in Budapest in 1905, but in Washington, five years later, the Americans saw to it that the question led all others—and that the decision this time went their way.

Quite fascinating, in retrospect, is the consummate ability of the American penologists, making excellent use of the kind of self-righteousness found in the above-quoted statement by Barrows, to convince the Europeans that theirs was the way of hidebound tradition, while ours was the only path along which decent and well-intentioned men could possibly proceed. This kind of propaganda can readily be pinpointed in the present volume when, for instance, Eugene Smith observes that "the theory of the indeterminate sentence seems to have attained at last the ideal of justice, after which the criminal law has for ages been striving . . . not only justice but mercy in the form of Christian benevolence." Rather like a schoolmaster patiently lecturing some vexatiously slow pupils, Smith further spells out the lesson:

> It will still require time to educate public opinion to full acceptance of the belief that the true aim of imprisonment is not to inflict retributive suffering upon the prisoner, but to make him fit for freedom; that the imprisonment should continue until that aim is accomplished, no matter how long it may take, and no matter what the prisoner's crime may have been; that, in perfect analogy to a hospital or an insane asylum, a prison is only a sanitarium where every inmate must be retained and treated until he is cured and can safely be discharged. The indeterminate sentence without limits cannot be adopted, in fact, until these beliefs have supplanted the ancient ones and have become thoroughly grounded in the public mind.

These arguments by Eugene Smith undoubtedly made some converts. Shrewdly, the Americans also had scheduled a nationwide tour of correctional facilities for the foreign delegates, to precede the convention. The first stop, of course, was the Elmira Reformatory. There the foreign visitors were personally escorted about by Brockway, the leading proponent of the indeterminate sentence. The trip led one of the most astute of the delegates, Adolphe Prins of Belgium, to some philosophical musing, and the results of his soul-searching bear witness to the manner in which the Americans had gotten others to accept their definition of the situation:

> The difference between America and Europe results from [many] causes: in the first place, from the pessimism of our civilization, which distrusts the criminal, because we have not room enough for our respectable classes, and furthermore, from the optimism of the new world, which does not distrust the criminal, because all men available can be made useful, even criminals.

Prins was not, however, totally taken in by the new ways, despite the fact that he was obviously charmed and not a little overwhelmed by the ebullience of the New World. In the United States, he wrote, "the old system is replaced by the enthusiastic, superstitious, exaggerated faith in the effect of education upon the convict." Nor was the cross-country tour an unqualified success. "The only thing to do with the Tombs," an English delegate told newspaper reporters after a visit to the New York City jail, "is to tear it down." That the Tombs remains operative sixty years after this condemnation, and remains as vile an institution today as it was in 1910, provides some idea of the kinds of inertia against which Eugene Smith inveighs in this book as he calls for basic reforms in criminal law and the treatment of offenders.

Endorsement of the principle of indeterminate sentencing at the 1910 meeting of the International Penal and Penitentiary Congress became, in the words of an historian of the meetings, "perhaps the most revolutionary stand ever taken by any Congress." Eighteen papers had been prepared on the subject—more than on any other topic on the program. Opponents went only so far as to suggest that the idea might be fine for America, but that it would be retrogressive for some European countries. A Spanish delegate, for instance, noted that in his country it had taken centuries to establish the principle of determination and to substitute clearly defined, definite penalties for the whim of the executive in dealing with criminal offenses. Indefiniteness, the Spaniard insisted, was a characteristic of a tyrannical epoch.

But such notions could hardly stand against the exuberant ethnocentrism of the American group. The editor of *The Survey,* a leading American journal of opinion, provides an expression of the kind of arrogance and condescension with which the American delegation approached the convention agenda. First, the editor describes the performance of Charles Henderson, a minister turned sociologist who presided at the Washington meeting. Henderson, the journalist noted, "gave fire, dignity, and spiritual earnestness to the gathering." Not totally satisfied with this panegyric, however, the writer seeks to underline its importance by contrasting Henderson's behavior to that of others at the meeting: "In this Congress of eager, gesticulating Latins, there was something thrilling in the restraint of the American president."

The discussion about the indeterminate sentence at the Congress appeared to the writer from *The Survey* to have the following form:

> At the other end of the table was an equally quiet group of Americans, two professors, a prison reformer, two or three wardens— a little bit bewildered, looking like a group of business men at a symphony concert, but with an air that the points at controversy had long been threshed out among them, and that they were willing to let the others go through what was for the older countries a harder process of readjustment.

Given such conditions, the outcome of the debate was almost anticlimatic. Ten years after the 1900 meeting in Brussels had insisted that "indeterminancy was inadmissible," the delegates flatly reversed their position and declared that "The Congress approves the scientific principle of the indeterminate sentence" and that "The indeterminate sentence should be applied to moral and mental defectives [and] to criminals, particularly young offenders."

Interpreting this development, Sir Evelyn Ruggles-Brise, head of the British delegation, was, like so many others, prone to find its roots in the character of American society. "A conservative adherence to old methods and principles of punishment is hardly to be expected in a people so equipped with the latest scientific ideas, and by temperament so impatient of traditional doctrines," he wrote. Similarly, Ruggles-Brise found American advocacy of the indeterminate sentence an expression of kindness and compassion in the American ethos, precisely what to-day's critics of the practice, as we shall note later, find it *not* to be:

It will be asked then whether, in America, anti-social conduct does not give rise to moral indignation and a desire for a certainty and a fixity of punishment. Not, I think, to the same extent as in Europe. Firstly, the easy-going tolerance and kindliness of the race is proverbial, and there is not the same degree of moral indignation when rights are violated as in the older and more settled countries of Europe. Secondly, the idea of good citizenship, and of a high sense of civic duty, has a great hold on a very practical race, who regard so much time spent in prison under fixed sentences as so much value lost to the State as a going industrial concern. The criminal man is an unfortunate—the victim of circumstances. The prison authority and the Parole Board must rehabilitate him; the function of the Judge is finished when guilt or innocence is declared.

The issue of indeterminancy can be seen, in these terms, to constitute the core of Eugene Smith's presentation in *Criminal Law in the United States*. It is the section where he most moves from exposition of things as they exist to vigorous advocacy of a quite novel position. This is not to say that Smith does not otherwise tell you what he thinks, be it about the anti-trust laws (where his career as a corporation lawyer rather clearly relates to his economic philosophy), the state of criminal statistics, or the sentencing practices of judges. It is noteworthy too that Smith subscribes to a position not unfamiliar to today's critics of what they regard as excessive niceties in criminal court procedure, which they believe make it too difficult to convict the guilty. But lest it be thought that Smith's position is nothing other than a stereotypic conservative line it ought to be noted that Judge Louis D. Brandeis, a bastion of liber-alism, sometimes thought similarly: "There is danger that, if the Court does not temper its doctrinaire logic with a little practical wisdom," Brandeis wrote in *Terminieloo v. City of Chicago* (337 U.S. 1, 1949), "it will convert the constitutional bill of rights into a suicide pact."

Though it should be remembered by the reader as he proceeds through *Criminal Law in the United States* that it was written more than sixty years ago, by the standards of any period the monograph represents a carefully reasoned, well-presented, fair-minded, and artic-ulate piece of work. The writing style is outstanding—simple, clear, forceful—and the arguments strong. Smith obviously possessed a keen mind that had been well trained. His effort appears all the more extraordinary when it is recalled that he was writing at a time when correctional discourse most often took the form, in the apt description of Edward A. Ross, of "a turgid mass of stale metaphysics, dark sayings, random historical allusions and mawkish ethical raptures."

What, then, in addition to substantive information, can be learned from a backward look through some threescore years at this work of a refined, intelligent man writing on a subject of great contemporary relevance? I would suggest that one answer to this question has been encapsulated in another statement by Justice Brandeis. In *Olmstead v. U.S.* (277 U.S. 479, 1927), Brandeis wrote: "Experience should teach us to be most on our guard to protect liberty when the Government's purposes are beneficent. Men born to freedom are naturally alert to repel invasion of their liberty by evil-minded rulers. The greatest dangers to liberty lurk in insidious encroachment by men of zeal, well meaning but without understanding."

Look today, if you will, at the results of the establishment of the indeterminate sentence, the procedure so well argued by Eugene Smith as a form of "Christian beneficence," "social protection," and "justice." From the prisons in California, the state in which the indeterminate sentence has been most thoroughly put into practice, the following represent a sample of recent judgments:

From *Time Magazine*, January 18, 1971:

> Though it leads all states in systematic penology, California has the nation's highest crime rate. Critics also claim that the system is characterized by a kind of penal paternalism that becomes psychological torment. In a much touted reform, California judges give indeterminate sentences; corrections officials then determine each offender's fate according to his presumably well-tested behavior. . . . Because of indeterminate sentences, California "corrects" offenders longer than any other state by a seemingly endless process (median prison stay: 36 months) that stirs anger against the not always skilled correctors. Says one San Quentin official: "It's like going to school, and never knowing when you'll graduate."

From the *New York Times*, February 7, 1971, concerning the trial of the "Soledad 7," inmates of California's medium-security institution who are accused of murder and conspiracy to commit murder in the death of a guard:

> Even if all seven defendants are ultimately cleared, they can still face an almost indefinite stay in jail. All seven and thousands of others are imprisoned under California's "indeterminate sentence" law, which means that a prisoner's time in custody is decided by the Adult Authority, a special review board.
>
> "No matter what the courts say, if the Adult Authority thinks you're guilty, they can keep you in jail as long as they want," said

Patrick S. Hallinan, lawyer for the Soledad 7. George Jackson, for example, has already served more than 10 years for robbing $70.

This law, Mr. Hallinan believes, is as responsible for the ugly mood in California prisons as anything. It makes prisoners completely vulnerable to guards who can put a "beef" in their files and thus prevent their release. "It's a nightmare," the lawyer said. "In prison you have no rights, no protection."

A proper verdict on Eugene Smith and the indeterminate sentence might be that Smith clearly fits Judge Learned Hand's definition of the man imbued with the spirit of liberty, "that spirit that is not too sure that it is right." Smith grants that in 1910 the moment was not quite correct for inauguration of the indeterminate sentence, because the United States still lacked both the facilities and the personnel to make the system operate correctly. But he nevertheless diligently pursued his "beneficent" end, rather carried away by the chimerical hope that out of innovation, since it was motivated by good will, will emerge progress. But the indeterminate sentence, seen by its proponents as a method of quicker reformation and shorter sentences, has in considerable measure probably contributed to the fact that the United States today locks up more persons and for longer periods of time than any other country in the western world.

This, then, is a lesson that might be learned from perusal of *Criminal Law in the United States:* "Every form of social oppression," Thomas Szasz notes, "has, at some time during its history, been justified on the ground of helpfulness toward the oppressed." There are, of course, other lessons too, many of them related to the almost unbelievable resistance of the criminal justice system to change. Virtually all of the problems complained of by Eugene Smith remain unresolved: State criminal penalties continue to show a highly variegated, almost whimsical pattern, and sentencing procedures are, at best, erratic. The question of prison labor is still a quagmire, with probably as many as 50 percent of the nation's inmates totally idle, not by choice, but because of the absence of adequate work programs. And the recidivism complained of by Smith is, perhaps because of better counting procedures, even higher today than the figures which struck Smith in 1910 as incontrovertible evidence of the failure of the American criminal justice system.

Biographical information regarding Eugene Smith provides a backdrop for a better appreciation of the ideas presented in *Criminal Law in the United States.*

Smith was 71-years old at the time this book was published, having been born in New York City on April 24, 1839. His father was a partner in a firm manufacturing printing presses and, on the father's side, the family was descended from one Charles Smith, who had settled in Connecticut in the 1600s. Smith's mother's family, the Davenports, had been among the first settlers of the town of New Haven. Matthew Smith, Eugene's father, died in 1841, at the age of 33, only two years after the boy was born. His mother was to remain alive until 1910, her 96th year, and the year in which this volume was published.

Eugene Smith entered Yale College in 1855 in an atmosphere tense with the imminence of the Civil War. During Smith's freshman year, later Yale historians have noted, the campus was agog with excitement about events in "bleeding Kansas," where anti- and pro-slavery forces were contending for supremacy, with armed Missourians intimidating voters and stuffing ballot boxes during the 1855 Kansas elections. But students at Yale, then the country's largest college, were not quite as responsive to external events as their campus equivalents today. Indeed, the stringent regimen at Yale undoubtedly molded many of Smith's later views regarding proper training for criminal offenders. There were, for example, daily prayers at five o'clock in the morning, for which students, clad in the traditional boots and dressing gowns, hastened to the old brick chapel. Attempts to interfere with the schedule at Yale, in fact, met with stern rebuff. Thus, in the spring of Smith's freshman year, a delegation from his class called upon the president—Theodore Dwight Woolsey—requesting that he cancel an 11 o'clock recitation so that they could pay adequate respect to the memory of a deceased classmate. Once the nation's foremost Greek scholar, Woolsey had in his later years turned to international law, and now was regarded as preeminent in this area. But Woolsey was "aloof," "a stern disciplinarian," and the result of the petition was to be remembered clearly by the Class of 1859. "For that unique exercise of Freshmanic initiative," it was recalled at a class reunion almost half a century later, "the President forcibly remarked that the Freshman class should not be fully matriculated until ample apology had been rendered."

There were, of course, better moments, and perhaps one of the most informative concerns the improvisation of a 2-line song that would be echoed at each reunion until no living vestige of the Class of 1859 remained. In a way, the words—tritely embarrassing today—might be said to encapsulate the view that undoubtedly underlay to a great extent the life style of each member of the class. "The Class of Fifty-Nine, Sir," the song proclaimed, "Is Always Bound to Shine, Sir."

There were 107 members of that shining class of 1859. Graduation ceremonies lasted two days, and it was Eugene Smith who delivered the valedictorian address. It was titled, "Self-Discipline, the True End of Intellectual Exertion."

Smith did not serve in the Civil War, but 62 of his classmates were enrolled with the Union Army and 12 with the Confederate forces. Five of these men did not return from the War.

Smith was a loyal alumnus, and brief sketches of him can be found in the three anniversary volumes that the Class of 1859 put together in later years. At the thirtieth reunion, he is portrayed as a man filled "with fulsome emotions of youth," leading the Class in lifting up "a few wild Yale notes of the old time sort." He was one of 27 members of the Class present at the fiftieth reunion, where much time was spent in nostalgic memories of classmates now dead. Interestingly, one of the deceased was Henry Martyn Boies, author of two books on prisons, *Prisoners and Paupers* (1893), and *Science of Penology* (1901). Smith had been one of the contributors to a memorial volume prepared by Boies' widow, and his estimate of his classmate's work, as such things often do, seems to express his view about those things which he would like to believe could be said about his own efforts. Of the first Boies volume, Smith wrote: "Its conclusions are sane and logical, compelling concurrence; the spirit that breathes through the book is uplifting, optimistic and animated by an intense Christian faith." Of the second, Smith said: "Through this work, Mr. Boies is likely to exert an influence surpassing any of his contemporaries in moulding the thought of future generations with correct views regarding crime and the treatment of criminals."

By 1914, the Class of 1859 had almost ceased to exist, and Smith was one of the handful who contributed money toward publication of the final class record. That volume, read today, seems painfully poignant as the survivors of the Class of 1859 grope to find some meaning for their almost-completed lives. Ultimately, there is only the reassurance by the class secretary that the ivy planted between the last two buttresses at the northeast corner of the Old Library Building at graduation 55 years before continues to "flourish vigorously" and that "care will be taken to preserve its perpetuation" should any new building threaten it.

Smith's own career, following his graduation from Yale, took him to the Albany Law School, where he received an LL.B. in 1861. He then opened a law office in New York City and, almost immediately, as a philanthropic endeavor, became associated with the Prison Association of New York, as its secretary for some twenty years and then as its president for almost another decade. He was a rather prolific writer, with almost annual presentations at the meetings of the American Prison Association, and contributions to a wide variety of professional and popular journals. His writings tend to follow a similar format. He sees a problem, illustrates its ingredients and their implications, and then offers a solution. In a 1905 article in the *American Journal of Sociology*, for instance, Smith offers the view that criminal trials ought to be removed entirely from municipal courts and conducted only in courts operated by the states. As usual, however, he tends to overestimate the good that will eventuate from such a move, predicting that "inequities and inconsistencies" in procedures and sentences "would in great measure disappear." A 1911 paper delivered to the American Prison Association meeting points to the abysmal shortcomings of criminal statistics, and then suggests that the Bureau of Census be placed in charge of compiling a more adequate numerical portrait of crime, a suggestion that today, finally, is being given serious consideration by the National Institute of Law Enforcement.

Smith proved to be almost as long-lived as his mother had been. His death on April 5, 1928, just a few weeks before his ninetieth birthday, was noted in the *New York Times* with a 20-line obituary. His wife had predeceased him, but he left four children, two boys and two girls (one of whom, with memories of Yale, had been named Helen Woolsey). The *New York Times* obituary reported that funeral services for the deceased would be held in the Presbyterian Church, adding, ever so appropriately in summarizing the man, "of which Mr. Smith was a trustee."

Los Angeles, Calif.   GILBERT GEIS
June 1, 1971.

A Selection from the Russell Sage Foundation

Ann Greer
Consulting Editor

BROWN REPRINTS
Dubuque, Iowa

RUSSELL SAGE
FOUNDATION

CRIMINAL LAW IN THE UNITED STATES

By
EUGENE SMITH
PRESIDENT OF THE PRISON ASSOCIATION OF NEW YORK

NEW YORK
CHARITIES PUBLICATION
COMMITTEE . . . . . MCMX

PREFACE

The following chapters upon Criminal Law in the United States have been written upon the invitation of Dr. Barrows, the late president of the International Prison Commission, for submission to that body at its meeting to be held at Washington, D. C., in the year 1910. There are several admirable works, treating in detail the criminal laws of the various states and the judicial decisions relating to them, which are widely known and readily accessible. The present occasion calls for no such general and comprehensive treatise, which, indeed, the proper limitations of space also forbid. The object of the present writer is simply to present, from a penological point of view, certain distinctive and characteristic phases of the criminal law in the United States and especially those that, by reason of the dual form of government existing in this country, arise from the relations of the several states to each other and to the federal authority. Adverse criticism of the penal codes and of the punitive system in the treatment of crime must be regarded, not as a condemnation of institutions peculiar to the United States alone, but as an arraignment of the whole theory of retributive punishment for crime; a theory which now underlies and pervades the criminal law of all civilized nations.

The topics thus proposed are such, it is hoped, as will have a special interest for the representatives of other countries desiring a more intimate acquaintance with the problems incident to the forms of government in this country and with the prevailing trend of thought and effort now affecting the development of the criminal law in the United States.

EUGENE SMITH

NEW YORK, October 27th, 1909

v

TABLE OF CONTENTS

CHAPTER I   PAGE

Relations between the Federal Government and the Several
States... 1

CHAPTER II

Criminal Law within Federal Jurisdiction................... 14

CHAPTER III

Criminal Law within the Jurisdiction of the States........... 38

CHAPTER IV

The Punitive System of Criminal Law...................... 57

CHAPTER V

The Indeterminate Sentence.............................. 65

CHAPTER VI

Children's Courts and Probation Officers................... 75

CHAPTER VII

Criminal Procedure in the United States................... 94

INDEX... 115

vii

CHAPTER I

RELATIONS BETWEEN THE FEDERAL GOVERN-
MENT AND THE SEVERAL STATES

THE original thirteen English colonies in North America, when they declared their independence in 1776, occupied a territory that stretched a thousand miles along the Atlantic coast. These colonies had been founded at different times and under different auspices, and the oldest of them had already had a history of one hundred and fifty years. Their historical development had been on lines so separate and distinct that each colony possessed its own characteristic features, impressed upon the habits and pursuits of its people. Long distances separated those colonies that were the most remote from each other, there were few good roads, and the means of inter-communication then available were most meagre. Thus, personal acquaintanceship and social commingling between the people of different colonies was necessarily difficult and extremely limited. There was another reason which was adverse to the formation of community of interest and feeling between the colonies, and even tended to separate them more widely from each other. With these early colonists the struggle for existence was severe, and their main dependence was upon foreign commerce; in their efforts to foster foreign trade the colonies were distinctly hostile rivals, each against the others. Their intercourse with each other being mostly by way of coast-wise commerce, they came to regard each other as foreign communities, like the countries over-sea with which they traded. So, as the years passed, the colonies had interests growing more and more in conflict, which made their attitude toward each other one not indeed of positive alienation but of natural jealousy and rivalry.

The one, and possibly the only, bond of union between the colonies consisted in the common aspiration for freedom from British rule, and the only possible hope of winning such freedom depended upon combined action. They did unite in declaring their independence, but immediately after such declaration the thirteen colonies, each acting as before, separately from the others, proceeded to erect themselves into independent states; each state organized its form of government, adopted a constitution and body of laws, created public offices and filled them by election, and exercised the functions of a sovereign power. For the prosecution of the Revolutionary War, the states formed an alliance with each other, represented by the Continental Congress. But this Congress effected a very weak and limited union of the states, as its measures were practically dependent upon their adoption and ratification by the several states. To enlarge the powers of Congress, the Articles of Confederation were adopted by the states in 1781 and continued in force until the year 1789. It was still found that the central government was but a league between sovereign states, lacking power to enforce its decrees and to coerce the states to obey them. In the meantime, the several states had been concentrating their political energies, each in strengthening the organization of its own government and in developing its own system of laws, while so dull an interest was taken in the general Congress that it was often difficult to secure the attendance of a quorum of delegates at its meetings.

The adoption of the present Constitution of the United States in 1789 marks the really effective beginning of the United States as a sovereign power among nations. At the time of its adoption, the states, each in its separate domain, were exercising all the powers of a supreme government, hampered but little if at all by the Articles of Confederation. By the Constitution, a federal government was erected, with power to enact laws and issue judicial decrees which were clothed with supreme authority throughout the Union, any state law or judgment to the contrary notwithstanding. But the subjects and interests which were thus submitted to the exclusive control of the federal government were closely limited and defined by the Constitution; and all the powers of government which were not so submitted remained as they were before in the separate states.

"It cannot be denied that the sum of all just governmental power was enjoyed by the states and the people before the Constitution of the United States was formed. None of that power was abridged by that instrument, except as restrained by constitutional safeguards, and hence none was lost by the adoption of the Constitution. The Constitution, whilst distributing the pre-existing authority, preserved it all." *Northern Securities Co. v. United States* (193 *U. S. Rep.* p. 399).

To this distribution of sovereignty between the federal government and the several states is owing the existence of numerous systems of criminal law within the United States. There is, first, the federal system, confined to offenses against federal laws, which is supreme through all the states and pervades all the national dominions. Then, each of the forty-six states of the Union has its own distinctive system of criminal law historically developed, each system variant, and sometimes widely so, from every other system, but prevailing only within the boundaries of the state to which it belongs. And, finally, each of the territories and outlying possessions of the United States has its peculiar body of criminal statutes.

The theory upon which these multifarious systems operate has been succinctly stated by Judge Brewer in the case of *South Carolina v. United States* (199 *U. S.* 437):

"We have in this republic a dual system of government, national and state, each operating within the same territory and upon the same persons; and yet working without collision, because their functions are different. There are certain matters over which the national government has absolute control and no action of the state can interfere therewith, and there are others in which the state is supreme and in respect to them the national government is powerless."

Underlying and to some extent harmonizing these diverse systems is the system of criminal law embodied in the Common Law of England. The jurisprudence of the several states (with a few exceptions) is based upon the Common Law, which was, of course, the law of the original colonies. Most of the states, by constitutional or statutory enactment, have expressly adopted the Common Law, as it existed at the time when the Union was formed, so far as it was adapted to their altered situation and circumstances. Even the states of Louisiana and Texas, whose laws are based upon the Civil, and not the Common Law, have adopted the latter as a part of their system of criminal law. Generally, where the states have thus preserved the Common Law, offenses which are crimes at the Common Law are indictable and punishable although not covered by any statute of the state. The presence of the Common Law also serves to impart to criminal procedure and to the interpretation of statutes an elasticity and flexibility which promote the ends of justice.

It has been held that the Common Law does not enter into the criminal law of the federal government, and that no offense is punishable as a crime in the federal courts unless it is declared to be criminal by a statute of the United States. Still, the Common Law has been a main element in the very atmosphere in which the whole system of

3

federal jurisprudence has grown up and received its nurture. The Constitution itself refers to the Common Law and provides (7th amendment) that "no fact tried by a jury shall be otherwise re-examined in any court of the United States than according to the rules of the Common Law." The Supreme Court of the United States has declared that the language of the Constitution "could not be understood without reference to the Common Law." *South Carolina v. United States* (199 *U. S.* 437). In all courts, both federal and state, the Common Law is constantly resorted to for definitions of crimes, for construction of legal terms and for rules of evidence and of practice, in the absence of statutes to the contrary or in case of ambiguity in the language of statutes. Indeed, the fundamental principles at the basis of all criminal law in the United States are taken directly from the Common Law. Some of them can be stated as follows: the right of trial by jury; the presumption of innocence until guilt is proved; no prisoner can be compelled to criminate himself nor be twice put in jeopardy for the same offense; no prisoner can be convicted for an offense which was made a crime only by an *ex post facto* law.

The Judiciary Act, passed by Congress in 1789, provides that the laws of the several states "shall be regarded as rules of decision in trials at Common Law in the courts of the United States in cases where they apply." By the practical operation of this act, the forms of procedure, the rules of evidence and the legal remedies prevailing in each state are adopted in the federal court held within such state. The result is that the beneficent principles of the Common Law, which pervade the laws and the judicial procedure of the states, gain a controlling force in the courts of the United States.

By the division of sovereignty between the nation and the states, the United States Congress, in legislating upon the subjects placed within its jurisdiction by the Constitution, has the power to enforce its laws by declaring their violation a crime and to fix in each case the punishment for such violation. There has thus grown up a body of statutory criminal law enacted by Congress and administered by the federal courts. The principal matters to which these criminal statutes extend are impeachment and treason, frauds affecting the revenue of the United States, counterfeiting the coin, paper money, bonds or other documents issued under federal authority, violation of laws regulating commerce, cases of admiralty or maritime jurisdiction, infraction of naturalization and suffrage laws and laws affecting the post office.

4

The Constitution, in declaring the powers of Congress, specifies the power to define and punish "offenses against the law of nations." Under this clause, Congress enacted a law making it a penal offense to counterfeit the notes, bonds and other securities of foreign governments. The constitutionality of this act was upheld by the Supreme Court of the United States. *United States v. Arjona* (120 *U. S. Rep.* 479).

The Constitution declares that all treaties made by the authority of the United States (as well as the laws enacted by Congress) shall be the supreme law of the land, "anything in the Constitution or laws of any state to the contrary notwithstanding." The power of Congress to pass penal statutes defining and punishing violations of its laws has not been questioned; and, inasmuch as the laws enacted by Congress and treaties made by the United States (both being placed upon the same footing) constitute the supreme law, Congress, it is claimed, has like power to pass penal laws declaring violations of treaties to be crimes and defining the punishment therefor. In the absence of such laws, however, the courts of the United States are powerless to punish the violators of treaty obligations. The judicial power of the United States extends, it is true, by the terms of the Constitution, to all cases arising under treaties made by the government; but it is settled that no criminal prosecution can be entertained in the federal courts except for an offense which is declared criminal, and for which the punishment is defined by an act of Congress. The failure of Congress to pass criminal laws for the enforcement of treaty obligations has given rise to diplomatic embarrassments.

In the year 1891, a mob in the city of New Orleans broke into the jail and killed three Italians (besides other prisoners) who were confined there awaiting trial. By the treaty then existing between the United States and Italy, the United States bound itself to secure the same protection to the subjects of Italy within this country as that granted to its own citizens. Italy promptly made demand upon the United States for the punishment of those guilty of the murder and for the payment of money damages. The United States was unable to respond to the first of these demands. If the murder was in violation of the treaty with Italy, such violation had not been declared a crime and the punishment therefor fixed by an act of Congress; hence, the federal courts were powerless to act. The secretary of state made answer to the demand of Italy that under our dual system of government the murder was an offense against the

5

laws of Louisiana and was cognizable and punishable only in the courts of that state; he could offer to the injured sovereignty of Italy only the good offices of the United States government in urging the state of Louisiana to bring the guilty persons to justice.

The obligation to enforce the treaty rested upon the United States; with the state of Louisiana the kingdom of Italy had no contract, and the averment that the United States had not the power to punish the violation of its treaty was not accepted by Italy as a satisfactory answer. The Italian ambassador was recalled from Washington and the suspension of all diplomatic relations between the two powers was imminent. The incident was finally closed the following year to the satisfaction of both parties by the payment by the United States to Italy of an indemnity of $25,000. Whether the United States had any legal claim upon the state of Louisiana for re-imbursement of the indemnity so paid or for other redress, is a question outside the boundaries of the criminal law.

This occurrence, which excited wide interest at the time, is here referred to because it led to a discussion of principles which was most interesting and highly instructive, regarding the dual nature of government in the United States. President Harrison in his annual message of 1891 called the event to the attention of Congress and suggested the passage of an act defining and punishing, as crimes, offenses against the treaty rights of foreigners within the United States. An act designed to that end was introduced in Congress, and the constitutionality and expediency of such a measure were widely debated both within and outside of Congress.

The advocates of the proposed legislation declared that the New Orleans incident had placed the United States in an undignified and humiliating position before the world; that, while the Constitution empowered the President and the Senate to make treaties with foreign powers, it was a gross defect in our governmental system that the United States should be left powerless to enforce the observance of the treaties within the states and to punish their violation. It was urged that this defect could be constitutionally remedied by a simple act of Congress; that the power and the duty of Congress in this direction were clearly defined by those clauses in the Constitution which declare that "all treaties made, or which shall be made under the authority of the United States, shall be the supreme law of the land," that "the judicial power shall extend to all cases, in law and equity arising under . . . treaties," and that "the Congress shall have power . . . to define and punish . . . offenses

6

against the law of nations" and "to make all laws which shall be necessary and proper for carrying into execution the foregoing powers and all other powers vested by this Constitution in the Government of the United States or in any department or officer thereof."

It was pointed out that in 1845, Congress, acting at the instance of Daniel Webster, then Secretary of State, upon the occasion of a somewhat analogous diplomatic imbroglio, had passed an act under which the trial of a foreigner held in custody by a state court in violation of a treaty of the United States or for an act claimed by him to have been done under authority of a foreign state, could be removed from the state court into a federal court. By this act, it was claimed that Congress had already asserted its power to confer jurisdiction on the federal courts in certain criminal cases arising under treaties, but that the terms of the act were not sufficiently comprehensive. In further support of the constitutionality of the proposed legislation, reference was made to the fact that a foreigner, suffering loss and damage through a violation of his treaty rights, could by the express terms of the constitution bring a civil action to recover damages in a federal court; and it was argued that, since the constitution had placed within the power of the federal judiciary all cases in law and equity arising under the laws and treaties of the United States, it was a fair presumption from the whole scope of the instrument that it was intended to include jurisdiction over all crimes committed in violation of such laws and treaties. Finally, as to the expediency of the proposed legislation, it was insisted that, in the division of sovereignty between the states and the nation upon which the Union was founded, the whole subject of foreign relations was committed to the exclusive control of the federal government; that the power to make treaties logically involved the power to enforce them; that, when a foreigner within one of the states was murdered or criminally injured, the foreign state of which he was a subject, if holding a treaty with the United States, had a right to demand that the United States should bring those guilty of the crime to trial and punishment; and that the United States, in executing a treaty which it was unable to enforce, thereby incurring obligations which it was powerless to fulfil, violated the law of nations, to say nothing of the law of common honesty.

On the other side, the opponents of the proposed law took the ground that it was in effect irreconcilable and in conflict with our whole scheme of government, and for that reason was inexpedient and even unconstitutional. In the division of sovereignty between the

7

states and the nation, the maintenance of peace and order in the community and the repression of crime were left to the states, and to the states exclusively, except in those limited localities where federal jurisdiction prevailed; and with the state's orderly administration of its criminal law the United States was powerless in any way to interfere, save only in cases of riot or insurrection, which grew to be beyond the power of the state to control, and then the federal intervention was to be by military force and not by judicial process. The criminal laws of the state, thus administered in the state courts, made absolutely no distinction whatever between natives and aliens; they bound, and were enforced against, every person within the boundaries of the state, citizens and foreigners alike; they applied without discrimination to every crime, whether the victim of the crime were a citizen or a foreigner. This was our system of government, published and known to the world, and every foreigner coming here was by this system immediately placed upon an exact level with the citizens as to all rights and duties under the criminal law.

The treaty with Italy in the respect under consideration was as favorable to that nation as any treaty ever made by the United States has been to the other party; its language was as follows:

"The citizens of each of the high contracting parties shall receive in the states and territories of the other the most constant protection and security for their persons and property and shall enjoy in this respect the same rights and privileges as are or shall be granted to the natives."

The opponents of the proposed law insisted that our existing scheme of government did give the Italians in New Orleans precisely the same rights and privileges as those granted to the natives. In the same riot in which the Italians were killed, some citizens of the United States were also killed; but the murderers of these latter were amenable only to the courts of Louisiana, and over their trial and punishment the government of the United States had no control and the federal courts had no jurisdiction. On what ground, it was asked, was the United States bound to afford greater or different protection to foreigners than to natives?

The treaty, it was claimed, imposed on the United States precisely the same obligation that the law of nations imposes, in the absence of any treaty; the obligation, namely, to protect foreigners within its borders against crime in the same manner and to the same extent that it protects its own citizens. But no treaty or law of nations requires a government to subvert its established institutions

8

in order to provide for resident foreigners a different kind of protection from that it affords for its own citizens.

In answer to the argument that, as the Constitution gave the federal courts jurisdiction over civil cases in favor of foreigners, the intention might be inferred to give like jurisdiction over criminal cases in their favor, it was urged that exactly the opposite inference should be drawn; the fact that jurisdiction was expressly given in civil cases, while no mention was made of criminal cases, suggested the application of that canon of interpretation which is embodied in the maxim *expressio unius, exclusio alterius.*

It was further argued that Italy had no right to demand that the guilty persons should be criminally tried and punished; that the only basis for such a demand was the desire for revenge. But revenge is no longer accepted as the proper motive of criminal prosecution. Protection of the public, and not vengeance upon the offenders, is the only legitimate aim of all criminal procedure. It follows that the enforcement of criminal law is solely for the benefit of the people of the state or nation that enacts the law; it is a matter in which no foreign power has any concern or right of control.

It was alleged that the treaty-making power was itself subject to the Constitution and that the central government has no power to enter into any treaty which conflicts with that distribution of sovereignty between the states and the nation which the Constitution effected; and that the proposed act would be unconstitutional, because it purported to transfer to federal jurisdiction what the Constitution had placed within state jurisdiction.

And, finally, it was insisted that the proposed legislation, whether unconstitutional or not, was inexpedient and wholly unnecessary, because the existing scheme of government enabled the United States to perform all its treaty obligations by affording to all foreigners within the country precisely the same protection and security that are enjoyed by its own citizens.

The arguments urged by the opposition prevailed—at least the proposed act failed to receive the support of Congress and the measure was abandoned.

Within very recent years a case has arisen involving principles similar to those just discussed, which has excited world-wide attention. I refer to the action of the city of San Francisco in excluding from its public schools certain resident subjects of Japan. The case has been largely, but erroneously, treated as if it raised an issue of state rights between the federal government and the state of

9

California. The first, and indeed the only, question that the case presents is whether the act of San Francisco was in conflict with the terms of the treaty between Japan and the United States. If the act deprived the Japanese affected by it of no right given them by the treaty or by the law of nations, Japan had, of course, no ground of complaint. But if the act of exclusion denied any subject of Japan a right secured to him by the treaty, the act was, beyond any possible controversy, unconstitutional and void; void because in conflict with the supreme law, of which the treaty formed a part.

If any state, or any municipality within a state, should enact a law which discriminated between citizens and foreign residents, to the disadvantage of the latter, in protection and security for their persons or property, and declare its violation a penal offense; and should a resident subject of a foreign power holding a treaty with the United States (of the "most highly favored nation" class), be indicted in the state court for violating such a law, he could obtain a writ of habeas corpus from a federal court (under the Act of 1845 mentioned above), which would afford complete redress. But the law would unquestionably be held void by any court, state or federal, when invoked against a right secured by international treaty.

Other clauses of the constitution affecting federal jurisdiction in criminal cases are the following:

(Art. I, Sec. 3) 6. The Senate shall have the sole power to try all impeachments. When sitting for that purpose they shall be on oath or affirmation. When the President of the United States is tried, the chief justice shall preside; and no person shall be convicted without the concurrence of two-thirds of the members present.

7. Judgment, in cases of impeachment, shall not extend further than to removal from office and disqualification to hold and enjoy any office of power, trust or profit, under the United States; but the party convicted shall nevertheless be liable and subject to indictment, trial, judgment and punishment, according to law.

(Art. I, Sec. 8). The Congress shall have power . . .

17. To exercise exclusive legislation in all cases whatsoever over such district (not exceeding ten miles square) as may, by cession of particular states and the acceptance of Congress, become the seat of government of the United States; and to exercise like authority over all places purchased by the consent of the legislature of the state, in which the same shall be, for

the erection of forts, magazines, arsenals, dockyards, and other needful buildings.

(Art. I, Sec. 9.)   No bill of attainder or *ex post facto* law shall be passed.

(Art. III, Sec. 2) 3.   The trial of all crimes, except in cases of impeachment, shall be by jury; and such trials shall be held in the state where the said crimes shall have been committed; but when not committed within any state the trial shall be at such place or places as the Congress may by law have directed.

(Art. III, Sec. 3) 1.   Treason against the United States shall consist only in levying war against them or in adhering to their enemies, giving them aid and comfort.   No person shall be convicted of treason unless on the testimony of two witnesses to the same overt act, or on confession in open court.

2. The Congress shall have power to declare the punishment of treason, but no attainder of treason shall work corruption of blood or forfeiture, except during the life of the person attainted.

(Art. IV, Sec. 2) 2.   A person charged, in any state, with treason, felony or other crime, who shall flee from justice and be found in another state, shall, on demand of the executive authority of the state from which he fled, be delivered up, to be removed to the state having jurisdiction of the crime.

(Amendments Art. V.)   No person shall be held to answer for a capital or otherwise infamous crime, unless on a presentment or indictment of a grand jury, except in cases arising in the land or naval forces, or in the militia when in actual service in time of war or public danger; nor shall any person be subject for the same offense to be twice put in jeopardy of life or limb; nor shall be compelled in any criminal case to be a witness against himself; nor be deprived of life, liberty or property, without due process of law; nor shall private property be taken for public use without just compensation.

(Id. Art. VI.)   In all criminal prosecutions, the accused shall enjoy the right to a speedy and public trial by an impartial jury of the state and district wherein the crime shall have been committed, which district shall have been previously ascertained by law; and to be informed of the nature and cause of the accusation; to be confronted with the witnesses against him; to have compulsory process for obtaining witnesses in his favor; and to have the assistance of counsel for his defence.

(Id. Art. VIII.) Excessive bail shall not be required, nor excessive fines imposed, nor cruel and unusual punishments inflicted.

It will be observed that the Constitution, so far as it regulates criminal procedure, closely follows the lines of the Common Law.

Within the District of Columbia, the United States has sole and exclusive jurisdiction, and there all law, criminal as well as civil, is of federal enactment. So, within military reservations, forts and other places owned by the United States and upon American vessels on the high seas the federal government has, generally, civil and criminal jurisdiction. But within the states, the scope of the criminal law administered by the federal courts is narrow and closely limited. The subjects to which federal authority is constitutionally restricted are of national import and affect the people at the points where they come into contact with federal institutions. It is the law of the states, and not of the nation, that is in constant touch with the common life of all the people; it is ever present, regulating the acts of every individual, in so far as such acts affect others or bear relation to the community at large, and its protecting and restraining power guards the peace and order of society. Hence the great volume of crime in the United States consists of offenses against state law. Some offenses, indeed, that are made criminal by federal law are also included within those prohibited by state law, the offender being thus liable to trial and conviction in the courts of both the nation and the state.

The relation to be borne by the laws of the states to those of the federal government was anticipated at the time of the adoption of the Constitution by James Madison, in the following language:

"The powers delegated by the proposed constitution to the federal government are few and defined; those which are to remain in the state government are numerous and indefinite. The former will be exercised principally on external objects, as war, peace, negotiation, and foreign commerce, with which last the power of taxation will for the most part be connected. The powers reserved to the several states will extend to all the objects which, in the ordinary course of affairs, concern the lives, liberties and properties of the people, and the internal order, improvement and prosperity of the state."

This anticipation has been substantially realized; but it will be observed that President Madison, in forecasting the scope of the federal government, specified foreign commerce as one of the principal objects within its power of control and inter-state commerce was not even mentioned; probably it was not then imagined that *internal* commerce was destined greatly to transcend foreign commerce in its magnitude and importance. The Constitution, however, expressly empowers Congress "to regulate commerce with foreign nations and among the several states." This power, so far as it affected inter-state commerce, remained largely in abeyance until two statutes were enacted by Congress, one known as the Inter-State Commerce Law, passed in 1887, and the other as the Anti-Trust Law, passed in 1890. These acts as penal statutes will receive detailed consideration in the next chapter. They have exerted a drastic influence upon commercial trade, and indeed have affected, directly or indirectly, all business enterprises throughout the Union. They have so extended federal control over interests which were formerly subject to state legislation that President Madison's interpretation of the Constitution as to the relative extent of state and federal power, may now require modification; it is at least doubtful whether it can still be said that the powers delegated by the Constitution to the federal government are "exercised principally on external objects."

CHAPTER II

CRIMINAL LAW WITHIN FEDERAL JURISDICTION

FEDERAL COURTS

THE Constitution provides that "the judicial power of the United States shall be vested in one Supreme Court and in such inferior courts as the Congress may, from time to time, ordain and establish;" and, among the powers of Congress, specified in Article I, Section 8, of the Constitution, is power "to constitute tribunals inferior to the Supreme Court." By acts of Congress, passed pursuant to these constitutional provisions, the United States is now divided into nine judicial circuits, each circuit embracing from three to twelve states. Each circuit is subdivided into judicial districts. A judicial district comprises in no case more than a single state and many of the larger and more populous states are divided into several judicial districts. There are in all the states seventy-seven judicial districts, in each of which is established a United States district court presided over by one or more judges appointed by federal authority. In each of the nine circuits are one United States circuit court and one circuit court of appeals, having two, three or four circuit judges, and presided over by one of the justices of the Supreme Court of the United States. Throughout the states, the circuit courts hold periodical sessions within each of the districts included in the circuit, so that every district has both a circuit and a district court.

JURISDICTION OF FEDERAL COURTS

The criminal jurisdiction of the circuit courts and the district courts is limited territorially to crimes against federal statutes committed within the circuit or district to which each court respectively belongs, except that crimes committed on the high seas or in places outside state jurisdiction may be prosecuted in the judicial district or circuit where the offender is apprehended or first brought. There are certain criminal cases defined by statute in which the circuit courts and district courts have concurrent jurisdiction; but in all other criminal cases, including the trial of capital offenses (except

14

as otherwise provided by law), the circuit courts have exclusive jurisdiction. Appeals from both courts can be carried to the circuit court of appeals but no further, except that appeals in capital cases can be taken directly to the Supreme Court.

The Supreme Court of the United States, with a chief justice and eight associate justices, has original jurisdiction in all cases affecting ambassadors or other public ministers and consuls and in those in which a state is a party. In all the other cases specified in the Constitution its jurisdiction is appellate; appeals may be taken to it from the circuit and district courts in certain civil cases, but in criminal cases the only appeal allowed to the Supreme Court is the instance (just mentioned) of capital cases. Appeals to the Supreme Court may also be had from state courts in cases, both civil and criminal, involving the construction or application of the federal Constitution or of laws of the United States.

CLASSES OF FEDERAL CRIMINAL LAWS

The criminal laws enacted by Congress may be divided into two separate classes; first, those that relate to offenses committed only in places under the exclusive jurisdiction of the United States or upon the high seas or within the admiralty or maritime jurisdiction of the United States; second, those that are in force throughout all the states, as well as in all other places over which the federal authority extends. For convenience of designation merely, the first may be called "local," and the other "general," legislation.

I. CRIMINAL LEGISLATION, DEPENDENT ON LOCALITY

The land comprised within the present District of Columbia was ceded to the United States for the seat of government by the state of Maryland, and is of course under the sole jurisdiction of the United States. There are many other places, situated within the states, which have been acquired by the United States for federal uses, such as sites for navy yards, forts, arsenals, custom houses, post offices, court houses, prisons. The United States has exclusive jurisdiction over crimes committed in all these places, provided the respective states in which they are situated have ceded such jurisdiction to the general government; but the United States cannot acquire exclusive jurisdiction over any place within the boundaries of a state except by consent or cession by the state. Such cession has uniformly been granted by the states and its effect is the surrender and transference of all state criminal jurisdiction over the places in question to the federal government. The mere acquisition by the United States, through purchase, of land within a state, for government uses, creates no federal jurisdiction over such land; but when the state consents to the purchase the state courts no longer retain the power to try or to punish offenders for any crime committed upon such land, the federal courts having sole and exclusive jurisdiction.

The United States has, of course exclusive jurisdiction over its territories and insular possessions, where it has established courts under federal authority. But when a territory is admitted to the Union as a state, the United States surrenders to such state, within the state boundaries, jurisdiction of the same kind and to the same extent as that belonging to the sister states.

The United States has criminal jurisdiction, exclusive of the states, also upon the high seas. But this jurisdiction is confined to piracies and felonies and to offenses committed on American ships in violation of federal statutes. Its potential jurisdiction extends to all offenses against the law of nations; but to exercise this jurisdiction, Congress must enact statutes providing the penalties for such offenses and designating the tribunal for the trial of them.

In all the places (mentioned above) which have been purchased by the United States with the consent of, or jurisdiction over which has been ceded by, the states where they are situated, in its territories and insular possessions and upon the high seas, the United States has sole jurisdiction over all crimes committed; and this jurisdiction is exclusive, in the sense that the states have no power to take any action, or to exercise any authority, judicial, executive or legislative, touching a crime committed in any of those places. Moreover, the criminal jurisdiction of the United States differs from that of the states in one very important particular: in most of the states, an offense, even though not included in any state penal statute, can still be criminally prosecuted and punished, provided the offense is criminal at Common Law. In the federal courts, on the other hand, the Common Law of crimes is not in force, and crimes are purely statutory. It follows that a crime committed in a place that is under the exclusive jurisdiction of the United States wholly escapes prosecution, unless there is an act of Congress which (1) defines that crime, (2) fixes the penalty attached to it, and (3) declares the tribunal before which the trial shall be had.

This situation demanded from Congress the adoption of a comprehensive system of penal law broad enough and minute enough to protect the places within the exclusive jurisdiction of the United

States against every crime known to both the statutory and the Common Law of the country. This duty Congress surprisingly failed to meet. Very early in the history of the United States, in the year 1790, a "Crimes Act" was passed; it related mainly to offenses on the high seas, to treason, to offenses against neutrality and against the coinage, but it was silent upon most of the common offenses which make up the great volume of crime. The meagreness of this act is explained by the belief, then prevalent, that the federal courts possessed a Common Law jurisdiction; it was generally supposed that an offense which was criminal at Common Law could be prosecuted and punished in the federal court, in the absence of a specific act of Congress. This opinion was held to be erroneous by the Supreme Court in the case of *United States v. Hudson* (7 *Cranch Rep.* 32), which expressly held that the "exercise of criminal jurisdiction in Common Law cases" is not within the powers of the federal courts, and that "the legislative authority of the union must first make an act a crime, affix a punishment to it, and declare the court that shall have jurisdiction of the offense."

United States v. Hudson was decided in the year 1812; it placed the federal criminal law in a deplorable plight. There were numberless crimes which could be committed with absolute impunity in the large number of places located in all parts of the country that were under the exclusive jurisdiction of the United States; crimes that could not be prosecuted in the state courts, because the states had ceded jurisdiction of those places to the central government, nor in the federal courts, because Congress had failed to pass the requisite penal statutes. The remedy lay in the speedy enactment by Congress of a comprehensive criminal code. Such a code, it would appear, was drafted by Justice Story of the Supreme Court and approved by all the other judges of that court, but it was never adopted by Congress. This anomalous and fairly anarchical situation, relieved only by special penal laws enacted by Congress from time to time, continued until the year 1825. The second "Crimes Act" of the United States was then adopted; it consisted of twenty-six additional sections, which were mainly a codification, with some enlargement, of the previous legislation of Congress.

Both these Crimes Acts were defective in that they left many crimes unmentioned; indeed, it cannot be said that they pretended to present a comprehensive enumeration of all crimes, in the form of a complete penal code. But the act of 1825 attempted to cure this defect by a new section which practically adopted the penal laws of each state by making them applicable to offenses committed in places under federal jurisdiction situated within the state. The third section of the Act of 1825 is as follows:

"If any offence shall be committed in any of the places aforesaid" (referring to forts and other public places the sites of which had been ceded to the United States), "the punishment of which offence is not specially provided for by any law of the United States, such offence shall, upon conviction in any court of the United States having cognizance thereof, be liable to and receive the same punishment as the laws of the state in which such dock yard, navy yard, arsenal, armory or magazine or other place ceded as aforesaid is situated provide for the like offence when committed within the body of any county of such state."

This ingenious substitute for a national penal code was soon proved to contain some very troublesome and unforeseen defects. One of the earliest decisions upon the construction and effect of the section was in *United States v. Paul* (6 *Peters R.* 141). Chief Justice Marshall there held that the section "is to be limited to the laws of the several states in force at the time of its enactment." The penal laws of the states are constantly undergoing revision, amendment and repeal, new laws adapted to changed conditions taking the place of old laws repealed. Congress may have the power to adopt as its own an existing state law, but it obviously has not power to adopt in advance any amendment the state may hereafter make to that law, nor to delegate to the state the power to legislate for Congress in adopting a new substituted law in place of the existing law. The result followed that the federal courts might be compelled to punish crimes, if at all, by applying to them some obsolete statute which had long before been repealed by the state. It can hardly be believed that Congress originally intended that the act should involve the sentencing of an offender to punishment under a statute which had been repealed and was therefore non-existent. The Court said, in *United States v. Barney* (5 *Blatch R.* 294), "I should hesitate long, before deciding that Congress intended that the courts should resort to the repealed laws of any state as a source of criminal jurisdiction."

The decision in *United States v. Paul* and subsequent cases following its authority made the third section of the Act of 1825 inapplicable in all states admitted to the Union after its enactment, because the laws of such states were obviously not in force when the act was passed. Neither was the act applicable to any places ceded to the United States after its enactment. The law remained in this situation for a period of forty-one years, from 1825 to 1866. During this period, twelve new states were admitted to the Union and the number of places ceded to the United States and coming within its exclusive jurisdiction all over the country was very largely increased. And yet, during all this period, no crime committed in any of the places within federal jurisdiction, which were located within the twelve new states or which were purchased or acquired in any state within that period, could be punished by either state or federal authority, except the comparatively few crimes expressly covered by the acts of Congress.

In 1866 an act was passed by Congress which substantially re-enacted the third section of the Act of 1825, with two material additions: its provisions extended to all places which "have been or shall hereafter be" ceded to the United States, and expressly declared that the punishments provided by the state laws then in force should continue to be applied, notwithstanding such state laws might afterward be repealed by the state. This act adopted the state laws as they then existed, including the twelve new states admitted since 1825, and brought the situation fairly up to the date of the act. It also provided for places that might thereafter be ceded to the United States and come under its exclusive jurisdiction, but it did not extend to states that might be admitted to the Union after the passage of the act. But the provisions for the future which continued the application of a state statute after its amendment or repeal by the state, was prompted by the impossibility of Congress adopting in advance any change the state might thereafter make in its penal statutes. It was thought better that an offender should be punished under an extinct law than that he should not be punished at all, and this method was adopted in order to secure, in the future, punishment of all crimes, notwithstanding the changes in the criminal law constantly going on in the states, through revision, amendment and repeal. Perhaps no better method could be devised, if the plan of a national penal code is to be rejected. Still, public sentiment will always revolt at a sentence of condemnation based upon a statute that has no legal existence. To avoid this result, the act of Congress should be frequently re-enacted and so keep pace with the progress of state penal legislation.

The Act of 1866 has been substantially re-enacted, in the Revised Statutes of the United States, in an act passed in 1898 and in the present penal code of the laws of the United States adopted in 1909.

The relation borne by federal jurisprudence to the penal laws of the several states therefore remains the same now as it was when originally created by the third section of the Act of 1825.

A FEDERAL PENAL CODE

For reasons which have already been made apparent, urgent demands have been made upon Congress, during the last hundred years, for the adoption of a national penal code which should be wholly independent of state laws. Congress has always manifested reluctance to take this step. The reluctance may be accounted for partly by consideration of the fundamental plan of our government, according to which the maintenance of public order and the punishment of crime were peculiarly matters of state supervision and control. The body of criminal laws in a state represents the stage of civilization reached by the people of the state and reflects the prevailing moral sentiments of the community. It is the merest truism that a criminal law cannot be enforced and has no value unless it is approved and supported by the moral sense of the people. There is force in the argument, that each community (for a people scattered over so large a country as the United States) can be best governed by the penal laws of its own making rather than by a single and unvarying national code of criminal law. When we consider the different habits and usages prevailing among the widely separated communities that compose our population of over eighty millions living in different climates from Alaska to Florida, some states distant thousands of miles from other states; when we consider that the central government has exclusive dominion over places situated within every one of these states and that a national penal code, if made independent of state law, would have to cover not only every grave crime but every petty misdemeanor condemned by some city ordinance and would have to be made uniform in its application throughout all the vast dominions of the United States, we can well understand that Congress should stand aghast before so colossal an undertaking. It may be matter of serious doubt whether the construction of such a universal code is feasible, and a matter of more serious doubt whether the present system, crude as it may seem, does not produce more satisfactory results than could be attained by any possible national code.

Several such general codes, however, have been prepared and submitted to Congress but they have all failed of passage. Reference has been made to the code prepared by Joseph Story when Justice of the Supreme Court about the year 1818. Ten years later, a very comprehensive federal code of criminal law was prepared by Edward Livingston, who was then a member from Louisiana of the House of Representatives. Probably, no person then living in the United States was as competent as he was to perform this task. Edward Livingston was the earliest, and remains one of the foremost, among the penologists this country has produced. His most celebrated work was the penal code which he prepared for the state of Louisiana, with an accompanying volume commenting upon its provisions. The whole work was a masterly presentation and discussion of the principles and aims of criminal law and of the methods that should control the public treatment of crime and of criminals. It commanded wide attention both in this country and in Europe and is still accepted as a really monumental work. Edward Livingston was in advance of his time in advocating many ideas and methods, then novel, which have since been tested by experience and have now secured general acceptance. He became successively United States Senator from Louisiana, a member of the cabinet of President Andrew Jackson and United States Minister to France. The code that Edward Livingston prepared for the United States was most comprehensive: it comprised four parts, which were entitled, A Code of Crimes and Punishments, A Code of Procedure in Criminal Cases, A Code of Prison Discipline and A Book of Definitions. This series of codes was introduced in the House of Representatives in 1828; and when its author became a member of the Senate in 1831, he took measures to press its adoption but, upon his transference soon after to the Cabinet, the matter was postponed and finally abandoned.

The latest effort to secure a national code originated in an act of Congress in 1897 appointing a commission "to revise and codify the criminal and penal laws of the United States." The commission, impressed with the defects and inadequacy of the then existing criminal laws of the United States, decided to ignore them and to prepare an entirely new code based upon models of the most modern and advanced systems. Their first report was accordingly submitted to Congress in 1901 but it failed to receive consideration from the House. In 1906, a later report was submitted and referred to a joint committee of the Senate and the House. This committee then prepared a code of the existing laws of the United States, omitting redundant and obsolete enactments, harmonizing and amending the laws by reconciling contradictions, correcting omissions and imperfections in the text, and making such substantive changes in the law as they thought necessary and advisable. The code so prepared was finally adopted and became a statute of the United States in the year 1909.

There are some important features of this new code of 1909 that deserve mention. The specific designation of an offense, in the section defining it, as a *felony*, or a *misdemeanor*, has been omitted and, instead, a section has been inserted which declares that "all offences which may be punished by death, or by imprisonment for a term exceeding one year, shall be deemed felonies. All other offences shall be deemed misdemeanors." In prescribing the punishment of an offense by imprisonment, the maximum term of imprisonment only is mentioned; the omission to fix any minimum enlarges the discretion of the court. Cases often arise where mitigating circumstances exist in so strong a degree that the presiding judge may be convinced that a lighter sentence than the minimum fixed by statute ought to be imposed; the proper administration of justice is more apt to be hampered by a statutory minimum than by a maximum limitation. The code makes accessories before the fact liable as principals, thus avoiding the Common Law rule that an accessory could not be tried before conviction of the principal, unless both were tried together.

The death penalty is preserved in only three cases: treason, murder and rape. But in the case of treason, there is the alternative punishment of imprisonment for not less than five years and a fine not less than $10,000. (This is one of the few instances in which a minimum limit is set to the penalty.) In cases of murder and of rape, the jury may qualify their verdict by adding thereto "without capital punishment:" the person convicted shall thereupon be sentenced to imprisonment for life.

The traditional sentence to imprisonment "at hard labor" has been modified by omitting the words "at hard labor." There are two reasons for this omission, one theoretical and the other practical. Under modern theories, hard labor in prisons should be used as a measure of discipline and reformation and not as a part of the punishment; hence it should not be included in the sentence. The practical reason is that the hostility of labor unions to prison labor has controlled state legislation to such an extent that in some of the states "hard labor" is no longer found in the prisons. The central government has not established prisons of its own having sufficient capacity to receive all federal prisoners. Outside the District of Columbia, the United States has two national penitentiaries under exclusive federal control, one at Atlanta, Georgia, and the other at Fort Leavenworth, Kansas. To these penitentiaries, which are of quite recent construction, convicts are committed from the federal courts. Before their establishment, federal convicts were sent to various state and county prisons, under contracts between the United States and the various states or counties which owned and operated these prisons. By the terms of such contracts, federal convicts were confined in the state and county prisons, subject to the same control and discipline as applied to the state prisoners confined there, the United States paying a stipulated amount for their support and custody. The same arrangement now exists and federal prisoners are found in penal institutions under state and local control at scattered points throughout the Union. If an offender were sentenced to "imprisonment at hard labor" by a federal court to a state prison where hard labor (within the Common Law definition of the term) did not exist, he might be advised to apply for his discharge upon a writ of habeas corpus.

The new federal code has no provision for an indeterminate sentence or for discharge on parole. If the federal prisons had capacity to receive and did receive all the federal convicts, there would arise no legal difficulty in applying to them the indeterminate sentence and all the rules regarding parole as fully as these measures have been adopted by the states. As the situation now exists, federal prisoners committed to state institutions are placed at a disadvantage when compared with fellow prisoners convicted for the same offense by state courts; the latter have the inestimable privileges of the indeterminate sentence and release on parole from which the federal prisoners are debarred. The following extract from the Attorney General's report for the year 1894 sets out forcibly the remedy demanded. After referring to the reformatory methods of treatment prevailing in state institutions, the report proceeds:

"In these benefits and privileges juvenile convicts who are sent from United States courts have no share. Their sentences are fixed, and no matter how perfect their conduct, they can receive only such commutation of sentence as is prescribed for prisoners sentenced to prisons or penitentiaries. They are thus deprived, in large measure, of those incentives which induce others to work for parole, and the discrimination thus necessarily made results not infrequently to the absolute prejudice of the federal prisoner, causing him to regard his treatment as a species of injustice, and encouraging him in insubordination and discontent. To remedy this condition federal prisoners should be placed on the same footing in these institutions as the other inmates, and the statutes should be so modified as to

23

make applicable to federal prisoners sentenced to reformatories the indeterminate sentence and parole laws which govern the state prisoners therein confined."

Article III, Section 2, of the Constitution declares that the judicial power of the United States shall extend "to all cases of admiralty and maritime jurisdiction." Admiralty and maritime jurisdiction extends, in the United States at least, to all the navigable waters within, and along the shores of, the country; it embraces all the great lakes, navigable rivers, bays, harbors, inlets from the sea, whether included within the boundaries of a single state or of several states. This jurisdiction includes cases criminal as well as civil; and Congress is doubtless vested with such power of criminal legislation as pertains to admiralty and maritime jurisdiction regarding crimes committed on navigable waters located within the borders of a state. A number of such laws have been enacted (Chapter 12 of the new penal code of the United States), making it criminal to do certain acts "on the high seas, or on any other waters within the admiralty and maritime jurisdiction of the United States;" for example, when the master of a vessel inflicts cruel and unusual punishment upon any of the crew, or when any member of the crew conspires with others to make a revolt or mutiny on board the vessel, or when any person steals goods belonging to a vessel wrecked in any "place within the admiralty and maritime jurisdiction of the United States." These statutes would seem to be applicable to the designated offenses when committed upon a navigable river, for instance, wholly included within a state. They do not, however, divest the state of a concurrent jurisdiction since they are contained in the recent code of the penal laws of the United States, which provides (§326) that nothing therein contained "shall be held to take away or impair the jurisdiction of the courts of the several states under the laws thereof."

These laws, however, are in derogation of the general scheme of our government which leaves to the states the punishment of crimes committed within their borders. This becomes evident from Chapter 11 of the penal code just mentioned which is entitled "Offences within the admiralty and maritime and the territorial jurisdiction of the United States." The first section of this chapter declares: "The crimes and offences defined in this chapter shall be punished as herein prescribed: *First.* When committed upon the high seas,

or on any other waters within the admiralty and maritime jurisdiction of the United States *and out of the jurisdiction of any particular state*, or when committed within the admiralty and maritime
jurisdiction of the United States and *out of the jurisdiction of any
particular state* on board any vessel belonging in whole or in part to
the United States or any citizen thereof or to any corporation created
by or under the laws of the United States or of any state, territory
or district thereof." The clause printed above in italics excludes
from federal cognizance the crimes specified in the chapter, when
committed on waters that are *within* the jurisdiction of a state, and
leaves such crimes to be dealt with by the laws of the state. The
specific crimes mentioned in the chapter are murder and manslaughter, assaults, rape, seduction, destruction of human life by negli-
gence of the captain or other person employed on any vessel, mayhem,
robbery, arson, larceny and receiving stolen goods. As the laws contained in Chapter 12 of the penal code (mentioned in the preceding
paragraph), are part of the same act with said Chapter 11 and said
Section 326, it may be held that the words "out of the jurisdiction
of any particular state" must by implication be read into those laws,
thus limiting the broad language used. This view was taken in the
somewhat parallel case of *Ex parte Ballinger*, 88 *Federal Reporter* 781.

The disposition of the Supreme Court to preserve unimpaired
state jurisdiction over crimes committed on navigable waters within
the state is evidenced in the leading case of *United States v. Bevans*
(3 *Wharton's Rep.* 336). A marine in the service of the United
States murdered a cook's mate in the same service on board a United
States ship of war lying at anchor in Boston harbor. The murderer
was indicted and brought to trial in the federal court of that circuit.
It was proved that the water at the point where the ship was lying
was within the state of Massachusetts, but it was claimed by the
prosecution that the ship of war was a *place* under the sole and exclusive jurisdiction of the United States and that the federal court
had jurisdiction under an act of Congress which declared that if any
person should commit the crime of wilful murder "within any fort,
arsenal, dock yard, magazine or in any other place, or district of
country, under the sole and exclusive jurisdiction of the United
States" he should suffer death. But the court held that the word
"place" as used in that statute had a territorial meaning and did not
apply to a vessel lying in the harbor. The court, by Chief Justice
Marshall, used the following language:

"It is not questioned, that whatever may be necessary to the

25

full and unlimited existence of admiralty and maritime jurisdiction is in the government of the Union. Congress may pass all laws which are necessary and proper for giving the most complete effect to this power. Still, the general jurisdiction over the place, subject to the grant of power, adheres to the territory, as a portion of sovereignty not yet given away."

This case was decided in the year 1818 and has ever since been cited as a leading authority; it is believed that the acts of Congress passed since that date have not materially altered the situation as it then existed. The case is a very strong one in support of state jurisdiction over crimes committed upon its own navigable waters; for it would seem that if the United States had anywhere jurisdiction, absolute and exclusive of the states, it would be on board a ship of war belonging to the United States. In view of the language used by Judge Marshall, quoted above, it is extremely doubtful whether it is within the federal power wholly to exclude the states from criminal jurisdiction over navigable waters within the states. There appears to be at most a dual jurisdiction over such waters: one, an admiralty and maritime jurisdiction vested in the general government; the other, a territorial jurisdiction vested in the state and incident to its sovereignty over the waters as a part of its domain. This latter jurisdiction, if it can exist coincidently with the admiralty and maritime jurisdiction, has not been ceded to the federal government and cannot be extinguished by any act of that government.

II. General Criminal Legislation, Applicable Throughout the United States

The criminal laws of the United States thus far considered are local, in the sense that they touch offenses committed in certain places only, the federal jurisdiction arising out of a special relation borne by the general government to those places. The other class of federal criminal legislation (now to be considered) is general, having universal application throughout all the states and in all other places within the sovereignty of the United States. These are the laws necessary to enforce obedience to the general acts of Congress and to enable the central government to exercise the powers and perform the duties committed to it by the Constitution. They occupy the first ten (of the total fifteen) chapters of the new penal code, while the last two chapters relate to both classes of federal legislation. The first ten chapters relate to offenses against the existence of the government, against neutrality, against the elective franchise and civil rights of citizens, against the operations of the government, relating to official duties, against public justice, against the currency, coinage and securities of the United States, against the postal service, against foreign and inter-state commerce, the slave trade and peonage. The penal code must not be taken, however, to include all the penal laws of the United States. There are many acts of Congress relating to matters of civil law but embodying penal provisions for their violation. For example, Chapter 9 of the penal code is entitled "offences against foreign and inter-state commerce;" it omits many sections contained in what are known as the Inter-State Commerce Laws which declare acts done in violation of their provisions to be misdemeanors punishable by fine and imprisonment.

The power of Congress to enact legislation of this second class differs radically from the power to enact laws of the first or local class. In "local" legislation, Congress has exclusive and absolute jurisdiction and has the power, inherent in every sovereign nation, to enact any law it may deem expedient, subject only to such restrictions as may be imposed in the Constitution of the United States. But Congress can pass no law of the second class (designated herein as "general" legislation) unless the power to do so is given by the Constitution either expressly or by necessary implication. The powers of Congress in this regard are closely defined and limited by the Constitution. The same difference exists between the states on the one hand, and the United States (in regard to the kind of legislation now under consideration), on the other hand; the states have inherent power to enact any law they may judge fitting, provided it does not conflict with the state or federal constitutions or with laws or treaties made by the central government: the United States has no such inherent power and Congress must derive from the terms of the Constitution affirmative authority to pass a law on any subject not comprised within its exclusive or "local" jurisdiction. Another point of difference by which state jurisdiction over crimes is broadened is the fact (already repeatedly referred to) that the Common Law prevails in most of the states; while, in the federal courts, the only criminal law is purely statutory.

SEPARATION BETWEEN STATE AND FEDERAL CRIMINAL JURISDICTION

The stability of a dual form of government, as it exists in the United States, depends, of course, upon preserving the equilibrium between the separate sovereignties and the avoidance of encroachment by either upon the constitutional domain of the other. Usurpation is more possible on the side of the central government than on the side of the states because the United States commands far greater force than any of the component states to compel obedience to its decrees. But so far as the criminal law at least is concerned, the United States has shown no disposition to trespass upon the jurisdiction of the states. On the contrary, Congress has failed to exercise, to their full extent, the powers which are unquestionably given it by the Constitution to entrench upon state laws. In many cases where Congress had the constitutional power to take entire and exclusive cognizance of a subject, it has refused to declare its legislation to be exclusive, thus leaving to the states concurrent jurisdiction. Congress has refused (as already shown) to enact a national penal code that is independent of state law, and, indeed, has adopted the laws of the state for the great body of crime not covered by federal statutes; and even as to those statutes, it has been careful to declare that nothing contained in them shall be held to take away or impair the jurisdiction of state courts under the state laws. The United States has power to take cognizance of criminal infractions of its treaties with foreign nations, but, as shown in the preceding chapter, it has chosen to leave those within state jurisdiction.

If we turn from the action of Congress to the decision of the federal courts, we shall find in a still more marked degree the determination manifested to defend the jurisdiction of the states from federal infringement. The case of *United States v. Bevans* (just referred to) was one in which, it may seem to some, the Supreme Court almost strained the law in holding that the crime fell within state jurisdiction. Another instructive and leading case is that of *Tennessee v. Davis* (100 *U. S. Reports* 257). The defendant Davis was a United States collector of internal revenue in the state of Tennessee, charged with the duty of seizing illicit distilleries. While engaged in seizing such a distillery he was resisted and fired upon by a body of armed men; returning the fire in self-defense, he shot and killed one of the attacking party. For this act, he was indicted for murder in the state court. The case was removed to the federal court of the district; and a motion was then made on behalf of the state to remand the case to the state court on the ground that it alone had jurisdiction. The Supreme Court held that, as the defendant committed the act in discharge of his duty as an officer of the United States and in enforcing the authority conferred upon him by the laws of the United States, he could be held responsible for his act only before courts of the United States; that if a federal officer, thus acting, could be brought to trial in a state court for an alleged offense against the law of the state, yet warranted by federal authority, the operations of the central government might be arrested by the action of the state court. The jurisdiction of the federal court was upheld on the ground that the power of the United States to protect its officers in performing their duties was essential to the existence of the central government. Two of the Supreme Court justices, nevertheless, dissented with great earnestness from the decision, holding that the crime of murder committed on the territory of a state was an offense against the law of the state, and that the offender, whether a federal officer or not, was, under the Constitution, subject to the exclusive jurisdiction of the state courts.

One of these dissenting justices, Mr. Justice Field, by a singular coincidence, was tragically connected personally with a later case which arose in the Supreme Court involving much the same question. This later case (*In re Neagle*, 135, *U. S. Reports* 1) grew out of the following state of facts. One Terry, a resident of California, was interested in an action in a federal circuit court, Justice Field presiding, in which judgment had been rendered adverse to his interest. Terry, feeling greatly aggrieved by the judgment, conceived a violent hatred of the presiding justice and publicly declared his intention to kill Justice Field if he came to California. Soon afterward it became the duty of Justice Field to proceed to California to preside again over the circuit court of that circuit. Terry's threats coming to the knowledge of the federal authorities, the United States marshal in California directed Neagle, a deputy marshal, to attend Justice Field and protect him from attack. While the justice and Neagle were on the journey to San Francisco, and within the state of California, Terry made a murderous assault upon Justice Field, and Neagle, in defending the life of the justice, shot and killed Terry. Neagle was then arrested by a state sheriff on the charge of murder under the laws of California. Being brought before the federal circuit court of the district upon writ of habeas corpus, the court discharged him from arrest, upon the ground that Neagle, acting in discharge of his duty as an officer of the United States, was justified in defending Justice Field and could not be held to answer in a state court to a charge of murder based upon an act for which he had the authority of the laws of the United States. This decision was affirmed on appeal by the Supreme Court, but by a divided court.

29

The fact that in both these cases, where the decision seems so obviously just, there were long and earnest dissenting opinions, shows with what watchful and jealous care the Supreme Court guards the criminal jurisdiction of the state courts.

One of the latest cases in the Supreme Court drawing a line of demarcation between federal and state criminal jurisdiction is *Keller v. United States* (213 *U. S. Reports* 138), which held unconstitutional an act of Congress making it a felony to harbor alien prostitutes; on the ground that the regulation of that offense was within the police power reserved to the states and not within any power delegated to Congress by the Constitution.

THE ANTI-TRUST LAW

In federal legislation of the second or "general" class now under consideration, the two acts of Congress (referred to in the first chapter) known as the Inter-State Commerce Act and the Anti-Trust (or Sherman) Law are by far the most important. They invaded a field which had been previously left to the jurisdiction and control of the states. These two acts, passed in 1887 and 1890, have greatly increased the business of the federal courts on the criminal side. They were enacted at a time when the public mind was inflamed by hostility to corporations and especially railroad corporations. This hostility was by no means groundless. Corporations could be created, under general laws, with the utmost facility, and they were allowed to conduct their business with a free hand, not to say with a high hand. They were subjected in but slight degree to governmental regulation or supervision, and the visitatorial power over them, vested in the state, was laxly exercised. Commanding boundless resources of wealth and impelled by fierce competition, the corporations were prone to act with the arrogance of irresponsible power in the struggle to expand their business; they were often pitiless in crushing individual competitors; they made discriminations in rates which favored large dealers and ruined small ones; they were arbitrary and sometimes lawless in their regulations and their treatment of the public. They tended to monopolize the business of the country and it was claimed that these monopolies oppressed the people: it was difficult for a private citizen to enforce his legal rights in a contest with a powerful corporation and there were few private citizens who had the means and the courage to enter upon such a contest. There was thus widely developed among the people a spirit of bitter animosity and revolt against corporations and monopolies and particularly against what are known as "public service" corporations; there arose an insistent and angry popular demand that the corporations should be curbed and humbled and their lawless methods stopped. It was in response to this imperative demand that Congress passed the inter-state commerce and anti-trust laws.

But the power of Congress to intervene at all in this contest was limited by the dual form of our government. The corporations were created under state laws and subject to state jurisdiction. Commercial and mercantile business carried on within the limits of a state is under state, and not federal, cognizance. But the business of the corporations was rarely confined within the limits of a single state, and in so far as it extended into other states it became inter-state commerce. The Federal Constitution empowers Congress to pass laws "to regulate commerce among the several states." Under this clause of the Constitution, the laws under consideration were passed, but they are constitutionally limited in their operation to corporations and individuals in so far only as they are engaged in trade and commerce between the states or with foreign countries.

The provisions of the anti-trust act, so far as it bears relation to the criminal law, are contained in the first three sections, which are as follows:

Section 1. Every contract, combination in the form of trust or otherwise, or conspiracy, in restraint of trade or commerce among the several states, or with foreign nations, is hereby declared to be illegal. Every person who shall make any such contract or engage in any such combination or conspiracy, shall be deemed guilty of a misdemeanor, and, on conviction thereof, shall be punished by fine not exceeding five thousand dollars, or by imprisonment not exceeding one year, or by both said punishments, in the discretion of the court.

Sec. 2. Every person who shall monopolize, or attempt to monopolize, or combine or conspire with any other person or persons, to monopolize any part of the trade or commerce among the several states, or with foreign nations, shall be deemed guilty of a misdemeanor, and, on conviction thereof, shall be punished by fine not exceeding five thousand dollars, or by imprisonment not exceeding one year, or by both said punishments, in the discretion of the court.

Sec. 3. Every contract, combination in form of trust or otherwise, or conspiracy, in restraint of trade or commerce

31

in any territory of the United States or of the District of Columbia, or in restraint of trade or commerce between any such territory and another, or between any such territory or territories and any state or states, or the District of Columbia, or with foreign nations, or between the District of Columbia and any state or states or foreign nations, is hereby declared illegal. Every person who shall make any such contract or engage in any such combination or conspiracy shall be deemed guilty of a misdemeanor, and, on conviction thereof, shall be punished by fine not exceeding five thousand dollars, or by imprisonment not exceeding one year, or by both said punishments, in the discretion of the court.

The effect of the act is manifestly dependent upon the meaning to be attributed to the phrase "restraint of trade or commerce." The expression had a well-defined meaning at Common Law and, by a long line of decisions in the state courts, the distinction had been firmly established between contracts restraining trade that were lawful and those that were unlawful. If the contractor agreed with a competitor to abandon his business or trade and not to engage for the future in like business or trade, the contract was held to be unlawful as being in restraint of trade. But if the contractor sold out his business with its equipment and, as an incident to the sale and to increase the purchase price, further agreed not to compete with the purchaser by entering again upon the same kind of business for a fixed period of time and within a limited territory, the contract was not necessarily illegal; if the period of time or extent of the territory within which the contractor was restrained from resuming his trade or business were not unreasonably large and the contract viewing all its terms appeared to have been made in good faith it was sustained. The test of validity, established at Common Law and throughout the states of the Union, was in the reasonable or the unreasonable character of the restrictions embodied in the contract.

In the case of *United States v. Trans-Missouri Freight Association* (166 *U. S. Rep.* 290), the meaning of the phrase "every contract in restraint of trade," as used in the anti-trust law, received exhaustive discussion. It was held that the language must receive strict construction and that every contract which operated in restraint of trade or commerce among the states, whether reasonable or unreasonable, was made illegal. This decision was supported by five of the nine justices of the Supreme Court, but was strenuously dissented from by the other four. It was earnestly contended, in opposition, that the Common Law was always resorted to in the interpretation of statutes, and that where a statutory phrase was used (e. g., contract in restraint of trade) which had received at Common Law a clearly defined meaning, such meaning should be adopted in construing the statute. Stress was laid also on the title of the act which prohibited only "*unlawful* restraints." But the prevailing decision held that the "unlawful" restraints mentioned in the title meant the restraints which were made unlawful by the body of the act; that the term "contracts in restraint of trade" included, at Common Law, those that were reasonable and lawful and those that were unreasonable and unlawful; and the act under consideration, declaring illegal *every* contract in restraint of trade, necessarily included both reasonable and unreasonable contracts. On the other hand, it was claimed, and many authorities cited to sustain the claim, that at Common Law the term was applied only to unlawful contracts; that if a contract charged to be in restraint of trade was held at Common Law to be a lawful contract it was because it was held not to be in restraint of trade; and that, therefore, the term "contract in restraint of trade" always meant at Common Law an unreasonable and illegal contract.

If the word "unlawful" which occurs in the title had been inserted in the body of the act also, so that the act had declared illegal "every contract in unlawful restraint of trade," this discussion and the very serious consequences involved in the decision would have been avoided. The question arose again in *Northern Securities Co. v. United States* (193 *U. S. Rep.* 197), when Mr. Justice Brewer, who had concurred in the prevailing opinion in the *Trans-Missouri Freight* case and in subsequent cases following its authority, declared that in his opinion those cases were rightly decided for the reason that the contracts involved in them were in *unreasonable* restraint of trade. The anti-trust act, he further declared "as appears from its title, was leveled at only 'unlawful restraints and monopolies.' Congress did not intend to reach and destroy those minor contracts in partial restraint of trade which the long course of decisions at Common Law had affirmed were reasonable and ought to be upheld. The purpose rather was to place a statutory prohibition with prescribed penalties and remedies upon those contracts which were in direct restraint of trade, unreasonable and against public policy. Whenever a departure from Common Law rules and definitions is claimed, the purpose to make the departure should be clearly shown.

Such a purpose does not appear and such a departure was not intended."

If the *Trans-Missouri Freight* case (and the subsequent dependent cases) can be placed on the ground that the contracts passed upon were in unreasonable and hence unlawful restraint of trade (as asserted by Mr. Justice Brewer) then the position taken in the prevailing opinion—that the act embraced every contract, whether reasonable or unreasonable—becomes merely *obiter*, with the majority of the court opposing it. It may now be fairly claimed that it is an open question, still undecided, whether the act condemns any contract other than one in unreasonable restraint of trade and whether it was intended by Congress to go any further than to adopt the rule of the Common Law.

It can hardly be denied that the anti-trust law is an extremely crude piece of legislation. Its condemnation of trusts and monopolies is expressed in terms too comprehensive and sweeping. Besides *"every"* contract, it applies to *every* person, including individuals as well as corporations, and makes it a criminal act to attempt to monopolize *"any part"* of inter-state or foreign commerce or trade. If subjected to a strict and literal interpretation (and the decisions of the Supreme Court certainly point to such an interpretation) the act is calculated to paralyze all inter-state and foreign trade and commerce. Every person engaged in such trade *does* "monopolize" such *"part"* of the trade as he controls: and every legitimate effort he may make to extend his business is an attempt to monopolize a further *part* of inter-state trade. Such effort this law makes a criminal act. The *Northern Securities* case declares that the act prohibits the consolidation of two railroad corporations which compete with each other in inter-state commerce; it follows, by inevitable logic, that the act forbids the formation of a partnership between two merchants, competitors engaged in foreign commerce, and may even forbid a contract between these merchants by which one agrees to retire and sell out his business to the other.

It is only by large concentration of capital under centralized control that world-wide enterprises in trade and commerce can possibly be carried to success. The irresistible tendency of the present age in all kinds of business is toward the consolidation of resources and unified leadership. These combinations, if properly administered and regulated, instead of being injurious to the community, can be made to promote the highest public welfare; and they have now become so firmly established, their stock represents the investment of so large a portion of the people's wealth and is so widely owned by the poor as well as by the rich, that the business prosperity of the whole country is inseparably linked with the policy of concentration. To destroy these great combinations would mean universal devastation, would throw out of employment millions of workers and would cause a financial revolution the results of which, economic, political and social, it is impossible to estimate. It is becoming the sober judgment of the people that the regulation and control, and not the destruction, of this overwhelming tendency of trade toward concentration should be the only aim of legislation on the subject, and that the anti-trust law in its present form is a pernicious statute needing radical amendment; but the efforts made for its amendment have thus far failed to succeed.

THE INTER-STATE COMMERCE LAW

The inter-state commerce law is a much more voluminous statute than the anti-trust law. It contains numerous regulations, affecting the conduct of the business of common carriers, the violations of which are declared to be misdemeanors punishable by fine and imprisonment. By the original act, passed in 1887, and its amendments down to the year 1903, the individual trustees, officers and agents of a corporation engaged in inter-state commerce, who violated the requirements of the act, were made personally liable to the penalties provided; but the corporation itself in whose behalf and name they acted was not subject to criminal prosecution or penalty. In 1903, a law was passed which provided that every act of a corporation which under the previous law constituted a misdemeanor when done by a director or officer of the corporation should also constitute a misdemeanor against the corporation as well and subject the corporation to the fines prescribed by the act. In defence of this Act of 1903, it was alleged that under the previous law it was extremely difficult to secure convictions against the individual directors and officers; that the unlawful acts were committed by the corporation, which received the accruing benefit, and that the corporation and its property should justly be charged with the penalty. This change in the law has largely increased the number of criminal prosecutions against the offending corporations.

On the other hand, it has been urged that the Act of 1903 is violative of fundamental principles of equity. All the property of the corporation belongs to its stockholders, for whom the directors are only the trustees. The stockholders have no direct power in

35

controlling the transactions of the corporation and are guiltless and ignorant of any violation of the inter-state commerce law. If the law is violated, it is by the wanton act of the trustees and the officers and employes under their direction: they alone are the evil-doers and alone should be held liable for their lawless acts. Is it not a novel principle, the opponents of this law ask, to deplete the trust fund in order to make good the loss caused by misfeasance of the trustee? In reply it may be said that at every annual meeting of stockholders, a resolution is passed adopting and ratifying the acts of the trustees during the preceding year. The stockholders who vote for this resolution surely have no ground of complaint, for they have made themselves *participes criminis* with the trustees. Whether those stockholders who refused to join in such resolution and remain innocent of offense can compel the guilty trustees to make good the share of loss and damage that such stockholders suffer from the fine paid by the corporation, is a question in civil, and not in criminal, law.

What are known as the "immunity provisions" of this law have been the subject of serious criticism. Upon the trial of a criminal prosecution of a common carrier for violating the act, the trustees, officers and agents of the defendant may be compelled to testify and to produce any books or documents required, under penalty of fine and imprisonment for refusal. The act provides that no such witness shall be prosecuted or subjected to any penalty on account of any matter upon which he may testify or produce evidence (except for perjury if he testifies falsely); such immunity, however, extends only to the individual witness and not to the defendant corporation whose directors are thus compelled to testify. It follows that a corporation, charged with violating the act, may be proved to be criminally guilty by the enforced testimony of its directors who were themselves the immediate authors of the criminal act. But the corporation can act only through its directors and is held criminally liable for the acts of its directors because the directors are *quoad hoc* the corporation. Is it not an anomaly in criminal jurisprudence to compel a defendant to prove its own guilt?

Another result follows from this "immunity" provision that is violative of the principle stated in the Constitution of the United States in these words—"no person . . . shall be compelled in any criminal case to be a witness against himself." It is true that this clause in the Constitution relates to proceedings in the federal courts only, but the principle is universally accepted in this country as fundamental law. Many states in the Union have adopted statutes

36

relating to intra-state commerce quite similar in their provisions to the federal act relating to inter-state commerce. It is quite possible that an act done by a defendant in violation of the federal statute may also violate a state statute. Suppose that in such a case a corporation is prosecuted in the federal court under the inter-state commerce act, which makes both the corporation and its directors criminally guilty. The directors are compelled to testify (under the immunity clause) and their testimony proves the criminal act to have been committed by them and therefore by the corporation. The directors so testifying are personally exempted by the statute from penalty and from prosecution; but such exemption extends only to the federal courts, not to the state courts. Congress has no power to grant immunity from prosecution under state law. If these directors are subsequently prosecuted for the same illegal act in a state court under a state statute, their own testimony given in the federal court may be introduced in evidence, and they may be convicted upon the evidence that the federal statute compelled them to give against themselves. The act of Congress gives an immunity that is futile, and compels the witness to give testimony proving his own guilt, and upon that testimony alone the witness may be tried and convicted in a state court.

CHAPTER III

CRIMINAL LAW WITHIN THE JURISDICTION OF THE STATES

REFERENCE has been briefly made in the first chapter to some historical conditions which conduced to the development of differing systems of law, civil and criminal, in the thirteen original states. And in the thirty-three states that have been admitted to the Union since its foundation, the "sovereignty" of each has been demonstrated by the enactment of an independent body of law, with scant effort at harmony with the laws of the other states.

The resulting dissimilarity in the laws of the several states relating to the same subjects is the constant source of most perplexing legal problems. State lines have now been practically obliterated by the currents of inter-state trade and commerce. Goods are manufactured in New England upon contracts made in Illinois, the goods to be delivered in Texas; trans-continental lines of railroad traverse a score of states; a great corporation transacts business in every state in the Union; and yet on crossing each state boundary, every business enterprise encounters and is governed by diverse state laws. The conflict of state laws has thus come to be a serious incubus upon the industries and the prosperity of the country.

In the field of criminal law, one might reasonably look for greater harmony, amounting indeed to complete accord, between the laws of the several states. For all criminal statutes in all the states are drawn after the same pattern; all such statutes and all penal codes consist, and from time immemorial have consisted, of definitions of crimes and a statement of the punishment allotted to each separate crime. The aim of the penal codes has always been to graduate and apportion the punishment according to the degree of guilt involved in each crime; and this assumes the possibility of measuring the *relative* amounts of guilt that are inherent in all the various crimes defined in the codes. These degrees of guilt are expressed in terms of years of imprisonment, life sentences, fines or capital punishment; retributive punishment, inflicted on offenders and exactly appor-

38

tioned in each case to the amount of guilt indicated by the particular crime committed—this is the ideal of justice that seeks embodiment in the penal codes. It must be remembered that the criminal law of all the states alike is founded upon the Common Law; and that this same system of apportioning punishment according to the degree of guilt has prevailed for untold centuries. The conclusion would seem to be irresistible that (unless the system is essentially impracticable) by this time some consensus of judgment must have been reached as to the proper measure of guilt and of consequent punishment pertaining to the most common crimes. One might confidently look for substantial uniformity in the penal codes of a country divided into political states but inhabited by a homogeneous population sharing the same views and moral ideas and united in their interests and pursuits.

As a matter of fact, the very widest and wildest diversity and the most antagonistic conflict are found to exist in the penal codes of the several states of the Union. A few illustrations will suffice.

The maximum penalty for the common crime of perjury in the state of Connecticut is imprisonment for five years, in the adjoining state of New York twenty years, in Maine imprisonment for life, in Missouri death and in Delaware imprisonment for ten years with a fine of $500 to $2,000 and whipping with forty lashes.

The maximum penalty for rape in North Dakota is imprisonment for five years, in Louisiana, North Carolina and Delaware it is death.

The maximum penalty for incest is imprisonment for six months in Virginia, and for twenty-one years in Kentucky.

The maximum penalty for bigamy is imprisonment for six years and fine of $2,000 in Delaware, and imprisonment for twenty-one years in Tennessee.

The maximum penalty for assault with intent to kill is imprisonment for five years in Kentucky, imprisonment for life in Michigan and death in Louisiana, while assault with intent to commit rape is punishable by imprisonment for ten years in Kansas and by imprisonment for life in Massachusetts.

The maximum penalty for grand larceny varies from imprisonment for two years in Louisiana to twenty years in Connecticut.

The maximum penalty for breaking and entering a dwelling by night is imprisonment for seven years in Arkansas and death in North Carolina.

The maximum penalty for arson of an occupied dwelling by

night is imprisonment for thirty years in New Hampshire and death in South Carolina; for arson with intent to defraud insurer, imprisonment for one year and fine of $2,000 is the maximum penalty in Alabama and imprisonment for forty years in North Carolina.

The maximum penalty for forgery in Delaware is imprisonment for five years, a fine of $4,000, whipping with thirty-nine lashes and wearing a convict's jacket as an outer garment for one year after discharge from prison as a badge of crime; and imprisonment for life in South Dakota.

It would be tedious to pursue this comparison further, but the same disparity between penalties for the same crime, as fixed in the penal codes of the different states, will be found to exist throughout the entire list of crimes. This fact alone demonstrates the failure of the attempt to measure the guilt of any crime; there is no standard of measurement, no means of computation, no general concurrence of judgment, and the inequality of punishments means the denial of equal justice.

But it may be said that the *maximum* penalty is seldom inflicted and that, in actual administration of the law, the sentences really pronounced by the courts in concrete cases may exhibit a harmony and consistency that are lacking in the codes, and thus, after all, equal justice may in fact be attained. The United States census of 1890 affords the data for testing this suggestion. It contains a table giving the average length of the sentences actually pronounced for each of the principal crimes within each of the states. The figures thus given indicate, it must be remembered, not the heaviest sentence nor the lightest sentence, but the *average* length of all the numerous sentences pronounced in all courts throughout the whole state upon persons convicted of the crime named and in prison June 1, 1890. The average given therefore extends over a considerable number of years. This feature is omitted from the census of 1904 but there is no reason to suppose that the figures of 1890 are not substantially applicable to the present time.

The average sentence for the crime of perjury was ten years in Florida and one year in Maine.

For rape, thirty-three and one-half years in New Mexico and two years in Louisiana.

For incest, fifteen years in Louisiana and one year in Pennsylvania.

For bigamy, four and one-quarter years in Minnesota and four months in Montana.

For assaults, eleven years in Nevada and four months in the District of Columbia.

For grand larceny, ten years in Delaware and ten months in the District of Columbia.

For burglary, eight and one-third years in Georgia and one year and three months in Rhode Island.

For arson, seventeen and one-half years in Rhode Island and two years in Arkansas.

For forgery, seven years in New York and one and one-half years in Arizona.

The same diversity of judgment, in estimating the degree of guilt manifested by the commission of any given crime, exists among the judges who deal with concrete cases not less than among the legislators who enact general statutes.

The statistics thus far cited prove that there is no common standard of measurement to fix the just amount of punishment for any one crime. But the difficulty is greatly increased when the attempt is made to determine and compare the relative guilt of different crimes and to weigh one crime against other crimes bearing no relation to it. This, however, the penal codes, which assume to affix to every crime its just punishment, are forced to undertake; and the result yields further proof of the impracticability and positive absurdity of the attempt to reach justice through a computation of relative degrees of guilt measured by the maximum penalties in different codes. Many striking comparisons are found in the appendix to the census of 1890, from which a few only are here cited.

The guilt of counterfeiting in Ohio and Minnesota is twice that of perjury, but in Rhode Island and Alabama the guilt of perjury is twice that of counterfeiting.

The guilt of perjury in Indiana is to that of incest as twenty-one to five, but in Kentucky the guilt of incest is to that of perjury as twenty-one to five.

In Virginia the maximum penalty for bigamy is sixteen times that for incest, but in Wyoming and Colorado the maximum penalty for incest is ten times that for bigamy.

The guilt of mayhem in Ohio is twice that of burglary, but in Michigan the guilt of burglary is twice that of mayhem.

The guilt of arson in Pennsylvania is twice that of burglary, but in Connecticut the guilt of burglary is twice that of arson.

The guilt of forgery in Kansas is four times that of larceny, but in Connecticut the guilt of larceny is four times that of forgery.

41

The irrational and absurd character of the theory upon which all criminal laws are constructed can receive no more conclusive demonstration than that yielded by a comparison of the penal codes of the different states of the Union. The impossibility of measuring crimes by their supposed guiltiness and the damaging results that flow from the attempt to do so, together with the only logical cure for these evils, are more fully treated in subsequent chapters entitled The Punitive System and The Indeterminate Sentence.

The bad results of these conflicting systems would not be so injurious if the states were inhabited by separate nations having no organic connection with each other, like the distinct nationalities occupying the continents of Europe and South America; but the people of the United States are so united by community of sentiments and pursuits that the affairs of each state are followed with keen interest by the rest. The newspaper press devotes especial attention to crime, searching through the length and breadth of the Union for circumstantial accounts of crimes committed and giving full reports of notable criminal trials. The inequalities of the penal codes thus publicly exhibited cannot fail to excite derision and contempt; the claim of the criminal law that it dispenses equal justice is proved a false pretense. It is often said that reverence for law is one of the main bulwarks of civilization. How can the people revere a criminal law embodied in penal codes that are in irreconcilable conflict with each other, that rest upon no rational basis, and that administer punishments which are grossly unequal and hence grossly unjust?

It would be interesting to know what effect these diverse punishments have upon the volume of crime. Does the severer punishment increase or diminish the number of crimes committed? Unfortunately, there are no statistics complete enough to furnish a satisfactory answer to the question; but so far as the statistics we have throw any light upon the subject, they seem to indicate an *increased* prevalence of a given crime within the state which punishes that crime with inordinate severity. If this is true, it would serve to confirm the prevailing opinion that the penal law exerts only a slight deterrence upon criminals. The fear of punishment does doubtless have a restraining influence upon the non-criminal masses of men, but its deterrent force upon those addicted to crime is probably very limited. Excessive and unjust punishments tend, apparently, to increase the volume of crime.

While the conflict of state laws exacts more attention from the civil than from the criminal courts, there is one crime, that of bigamy, that is seriously affected (and indeed increased) by the diversity of the laws in the several states regarding marriage and divorce. The legal grounds upon which a divorce is granted vary excessively in the different states; in some of the states, adultery is the sole ground, while in others cruelty, desertion and even incompatibility of temper, are made a sufficient cause for absolute divorce. A husband or wife, desiring to obtain a divorce but having only flimsy cause for it, removes to one of the "easy" states, establishes a residence there and brings a suit for divorce in a court of that state. The defendant, living in another state, can be served with process only by publication and, not unwilling perhaps that a divorce should be granted, allows judgment to go by default. Judgments of divorce thus obtained have caused endless complications and trouble. This can best be illustrated by an actual instance which has become a leading case (*People v. Baker*, 76 *New York Reports*, 78).

Francis M. Baker was married in the state of Illinois to a resident of Illinois in the year 1871. After the marriage he brought his wife to New York where they established their home and lived together for a year or more. A separation then occurred and Mrs. Baker returned alone to her father's house in Illinois and became a permanent resident of that state, the husband retaining his domicile in New York. Two years after her return to Illinois, Mrs. Baker brought a suit against her husband in a court of competent jurisdiction in the state of Illinois to obtain an absolute divorce on the ground of "gross neglect of duty." By the laws of Illinois, "gross neglect of duty" was one of the grounds upon which an absolute divorce could be granted; by the laws of New York an absolute divorce could be granted for adultery and for no other cause. The defendant husband being in New York, process in the suit could not be served upon him personally in Illinois; service could be had by publication only and he was thus served in accordance with the laws of Illinois. The husband interposed no defense and entered no appearance in the suit. The plaintiff duly proved her case by competent evidence, the court granted her an absolute divorce from her husband, and judgment to that effect was duly entered in 1874. Mrs. Baker, having obtained such divorce, married a second husband in Illinois in 1875 and continued to reside (with him) in that state until her death in 1876. Such second marriage was valid by the laws of Illinois.

Some six months after the judgment of divorce, Mr. Baker also married again, being still domiciled in New York. For this second marriage, which took place in New York, he was indicted in New York for bigamy. Upon the trial he pleaded in defense the Illinois judgment of divorce. In rendering judgment of conviction the New York court conceded that the divorce suit was regularly conducted in accordance with the laws of Illinois and was perfectly valid within that state. Mrs. Baker, being a resident of Illinois and within the jurisdiction of its courts, suing for the establishment of rights secured to her by its laws, was entitled to the judgment she demanded and by virtue of that judgment was effectually divorced from Mr. Baker and afterward became the legal wife of her second husband. But the jurisdiction of a state court is limited to parties and *res* within that state. Every state has the power to fix and determine, through its own courts, the legal status of its own citizens. But no state has the power to judicially change the status of a citizen of any other state from that of being a married man to that of being an unmarried man, unless such citizen comes within the boundaries of the former state and is there served with its legal process or voluntarily appears by attorney in its courts. It was held therefore that Francis M. Baker, not having been brought within the jurisdiction of the Illinois court, was unaffected by its judgment, and, his first marriage not having been legally dissolved *as to him*, he was guilty of bigamy. He was sentenced to state prison for five years.

This case involves some deplorable and confusing consequences. Baker remained the husband of his first wife in New York, while she was no longer his wife in Illinois or anywhere else. A marital connection that is unilateral only is as puzzling as it is anomalous. But *People v. Baker* has never been overruled; on the contrary, it has been consistently followed and approved in numerous adjudications and its reasoning and conclusions have been confirmed by the latest decisions of the Supreme Court of the United States. It is difficult to impeach or escape the logic on which these decisions rest. They afford a convincing illustration of the unavoidable evils resulting from the conflict of state laws. How to bring these laws into uniformity is one of the serious problems now confronting the American people.

The only constitutional method by which such uniformity can be attained obviously lies in concerted action by the states themselves. The state of New York took the lead in this direction by the passage of an act in 1890 (Sess. Laws Ch. 205) which created a commission to "ascertain the best means to effect an assimilation and uniformity in the laws of the states" and "to invite the other states of the Union to send representatives to a convention to draft uniform laws to be submitted for the approval and adoption of the several states." Similar statutes were passed by other states in response to this invitation and thus the body was constituted which is known as the State Boards of Commissioners for Promoting Uniformity of Legislation in the United States. This body held its first Congress in the year 1892 and has met annually ever since. It has accomplished some good results, but has thus far confined its labors to matters of civil (as distinguished from criminal) law.

Following the precedent thus set by the state of New York, the legislature of Pennsylvania passed a law in 1905 under which the governor of that state extended an invitation to the other states of the Union to send delegates to a convention to meet at Washington to consider the diverse laws of the several states relating to marriage and divorce. In acceptance of this invitation, delegates representing some forty-two states assembled in Washington at the time appointed (Feb. 19, 1906) and formed the National Congress on Uniform Divorce Laws. During that year, this congress formulated a proposed "Act regulating annulment of marriage and divorce" and submitted it to all the states, recommending its universal adoption.

The American Bar Association, the National Conference of Charities and Correction and The American Prison Association, together with other agencies, have labored to awaken in the public mind a sense of the evils that result from conflicting state laws; but while some progress has been made in the direction of uniformity, the progress made has utterly failed to keep pace with the increasing and crying needs of the country for harmony in the systems of state legislation.

Prison labor presents a difficult problem in this country. Labor unions have assumed generally a position of hostility toward labor in prisons, partly because they have regarded prison labor as wrongly competing with free labor, and partly because the unions are unable, by strikes or boycott or other coercion, to control or to affect such labor as is carried on in prisons. There is also a popular feeling widely prevalent that productive industry in the prisons causes competition with outside labor which operates unjustly and is distinctly injurious to the free workman. The public, moreover, regards prison-made goods with positive aversion, rendering it difficult to find a favorable market for them. These are some of the causes that prove adverse to the establishment of a satisfactory system of prison labor.

That any kind of productive work of value done by prisoners might be done by free workmen and diminishes by so much the amount of work open to free labor can hardly be denied. It must also be admitted that goods manufactured in prison and placed on the market come into competition with similar goods made by free labor. The practical injury done to the free workman by this competition may be so small as to be negligible; indeed, it has been estimated that the value of prison-made goods amounts to one-sixth of one per cent of the value of the total manufactured product of the country. Still, theoretically and technically, competition does, and must, exist. No useful productive industry can possibly be carried on in prison that does not, logically, compete with free industry. The popular error consists in regarding this competition as an injustice to the free laborer. It is the duty and the privilege of every man who is able, to be self-supporting; this duty is owed to the state, which has no right to support at the public expense any man who is competent to support himself. And yet every man who supports himself by his own labor comes into competition with the laboring class. Such competition is rightful and no grievance of which the laboring class can complain. It is difficult to comprehend how the public can have forgotten these axiomatic truths so far as to regard the convicted criminal as a favored individual, exempt from the universal obligation, who, by the commision of a crime, has earned a right to be supported in idleness at the public expense. Surely, no imaginable member of a community has a weaker claim upon the liberality of the state than the convict who has broken its laws and defied its sovereignty. One supreme duty the state owes the imprisoned criminal. His confinement disables him from seeking work; the state should furnish him the means of earning his support by his own industry. When the state has done this, the convict is placed in the same relation to labor as the free workman outside the prison and is invested with the universal duty and right to work for self-support. This duty is not weakened, but is rather heightened, by the fact that he has committed crime and his competition with free labor is as just as it is inevitable.

There are no principles of scientific penology more firmly established than those relating to prison labor. Labor is the *sine qua non* of reformation, but it must take the form of productive industry. Mere physical toil, as with the treadmill and the crank, is not conducive to reformation; it is debasing and brutalizing. It is desirable that the labor should be not purely mechanical but of a kind that may excite intelligent interest and give occasion for the exercise and development of skill. Such industries, moreover, should be employed as may be useful to the prisoner by furnishing him with the means of earning a livelihood after his discharge from prison. In a large prison, many diversified industries should be introduced, fitted to the varying capabilities and aptitudes that are sure to be found in any considerable body of prisoners.

These obvious requirements have not been satisfactorily met in many of the prisons in the United States, although experiments have been made without number. All the various systems of administering prison labor find exemplification in the laws of the different states.

That which prevails largely in the southern states is known as the lease system. The state leases out to a contractor a certain number of convicts for a specified term of years at an agreed price; the contractor assumes the custody and discipline of the prisoners, clothes and feeds them, and works them for his profit. They are generally confined at night in convict-camps or stockades. These camps are subject to supervision by the state, but the supervision is exercised with such laxity that the gravest abuses and cruelties have been practiced and have made the camps in many instances places of unutterable horror. In recent years, public sentiment in the south is being aroused by the exposure of these abuses, and there is reason to hope that the lease system may be doomed to early extinction. The system itself is wholly indefensible upon principle; the renunciation by the state of its responsibility for the care and training of its prisoners and the commitment of them to the mercies of a contractor to be exploited for gain, under circumstances which make reformation a mockery, are opposed not only to every principle of modern penology but to every humane instinct.

The practice in the other states of the Union exhibits large variety. The contract system, the piece-price plan, the public account system under which goods are manufactured by the state either for sale in the open market or for use in public institutions, and the employment of the prisoners on public works—all these systems are used in the different states, with frequent changes and variations.

The history of legislation upon prison labor in the state of New York during the past generation is interesting and instructive; it is somewhat typical, reflecting progressive changes in public sentiment which have taken place in other states as well. Forty years ago the contract system prevailed generally in the prisons of New York.

47

The contractor, a manufacturer of stoves for instance, hired from the state the labor of a certain number of prisoners for a fixed term of years at a certain price per day for each man. The custody, maintenance and discipline of the prisoners remained with the state, which supplied work-shops within the prison. The contractor furnished the necessary tools and equipment, together with the raw materials, to be used in the manufacture, supplied instructors or overseers to superintend the workmen, and sold the finished products in the open market. This system encountered bitter opposition; first, from outside manufacturers who complained that they were threatened with ruin because the prison-made goods were produced at so low a cost as to render competition impossible, and second, from those who were interested in prison reform. It was urged that the presence in the prison of the contractor and his representatives interfered with the absolute control that the state should exercise in the discipline and training of the convicts; that the labor of the prisoners, being mere slave labor, aroused no interest and offered no incentive; that the labor ought to be administered under the sole authority of the state as an education to the convict and as a means of reformation.

In 1884, an act was passed forbidding the extension of any existing contract or execution of any new contract for the employment of convicts in any prison in the state. The abolition of the contract system was followed by resort to the public account system, which had indeed been used to a limited extent for many years concurrently with the contract system. Under the public account system then in use, the state engaged in the business of manufacturing goods for sale in the open market. The prison was operated as a factory; the state provided the necessary working capital, installed the machinery, bought the raw material, trained the convicts to do the labor, and marketed the product at the best rates that could be obtained. This system also met with popular condemnation. The state, it was alleged, entering the market as a capitalist with unlimited resources and employing labor without paying any wages, was a far more formidable competitor than the prison contractor had been. The tendency of the system was to diminish the profits of the outside manufacturer and to reduce the wages of the free workman.

The resultant agitation led to the drastic Act of 1888 which provided that no prisoner in any penal institution in the state should be allowed to work at any industry where his labor, or the product of his labor, should be farmed out, contracted or given or sold to any person whatsoever. The passage of this law produced the absolute suspension of prison labor in all the state prisons, whose inmates were kept for nearly a year in enforced idleness. The result afforded a most impressive object lesson upon the value and necessity of prison labor. The convicts made most piteous appeals to their wardens for employment, for work of any kind; a large number of them became insane; and as the situation continued unrelieved, the spirit of discontent among the prisoners became so turbulent as to threaten positive revolt and riot. Public sentiment was aroused and public meetings were held in sympathy with the prisoners and in bitter protest against the intolerable condition to which they were reduced by the want of employment. This obnoxious law was repealed the next year after its enactment.

In 1889, the act was passed which was known as the Fassett law. This was a comprehensive code of prison law covering the entire field of prison administration. Its key-note was the reformation of the prisoners and the whole act was characterized by broad and enlightened views, though somewhat in advance of its times, which made the Fassett law the most admirable piece of legislation relating to prisons that had ever been enacted on this side of the Atlantic. Its provisions regarding prison labor (which resulted from a compromise between conflicting interests) were, possibly, over-elaborated. These were prefaced by the following section:

> Section 95. The superintendent of state prisons shall direct the classification of prisoners into three grades or classes, as follows: In the first grade shall be included those appearing to be corrigible or less vicious than the others and likely to observe the laws and to maintain themselves by honest industry after their discharge; in the second grade shall be included those appearing to be incorrigible or more vicious, but so competent to work and so reasonably obedient to prison discipline as not seriously to interfere with the productiveness of their labor, or of the labor of those in company with whom they may be employed; in the third grade shall be included those appearing to be incorrigible or so insubordinate or so incompetent, otherwise than from temporary ill health, as to seriously interfere with the discipline or productiveness of the labor of the prison.

The act provides for rules and regulations governing the treatment, discipline, education and training of the convicts, and for a strict record of the antecedents, the conduct, the progress and the failures of each convict, thus providing the means for an intelligent classification.

The labor of the prisoners of the first grade was to be directed with the sole aim of fitting them to maintain themselves by honest industry after their discharge from the prison; they might be employed at hard labor for industrial training and instruction only, although no saleable products resulted from their labor; but, so far as was consistent with the primary aim of reformation, their labor was to be made productive.

The labor of the second grade was to be directed primarily to secure the production of things useful and saleable, but secondarily to fit the prisoners for self-support after their discharge even though their labor was thereby rendered less productive.

The labor of the third grade was to aim solely at healthful exercise and the manufacture, without machinery, of such articles as were needed in the public institutions of the state or such other manual labor as should not compete with free labor.

The productive industries of the prisons were directed to the manufacture of merchantable goods which were sold for account of the state. The system resulted in heavy outlays for tools and machinery and in a vast accumulation of raw material and manufactured goods; it proved far from profitable to the state but it possessed the advantage of furnishing the convicts with constant employment at useful labor.

All this was radically changed by the amended state constitution of 1894, which contained the following section upon prison labor:

The legislature shall by law provide for the occupation and employment of prisoners sentenced to the several state prisons, penitentiaries, jails and reformatories in the state; and on and after the first day of January, 1897, no person in any such prison, penitentiary, jail or reformatory, shall be required or allowed to work while under sentence thereto, at any trade, industry or occupation wherein or whereby his work, or the product or profit of his work, shall be farmed out, contracted, given or sold to any person, firm, association or corporation. This section shall not be construed to prevent the legislature from providing that convicts may work for, and that the products of their labor may be disposed of to, the state or any political division thereof, or for or to any public institution owned or managed and controlled by the state, or any political division thereof.

The adoption of this section was earnestly opposed by many persons who realized the absolute necessity of prison labor as a means of reformation, While it was generally conceded that the work for public institutions contemplated by the section was ideally the best form of prison labor, serious apprehension was felt that a sufficient amount of this kind of work to afford constant employment for all the prisoners could not be provided. Stringent statutes have since been passed requiring public institutions (of the kind designated in the constitution) to purchase their manufactured supplies from the prisons, and making it unlawful to purchase them elsewhere, unless the prisons are unable to furnish them. It required years of preparation to adjust the prisons to the new situation; it became necessary to establish and equip plants adapted to the manufacture of a considerable variety of goods, to instruct the convicts in new kinds of labor, to regulate the supply to fluctuating demands in different lines of manufacture.

Many public institutions employ their inmates in making their own supplies, and it would be highly injurious to deprive these inmates of such labor. Various trades which formerly supplied the public institutions besiege the legislature with applications to except and exclude their trades from the prisons. The printers have been successful and secured the passage of a law in 1898 which declared that no printing or photo-engraving should be done in any penal institution in the state, except such printing as was required for penal and state charitable institutions. This law greatly restricted the field of labor available for the prisons, as the state printing and other public printing would have furnished continuous employment for a large number of convicts.

Upon the whole, the apprehensions entertained by the opponents of the new system introduced by the amended constitution have been fully justified. While it is claimed that the convicts in the state prisons are now furnished with employment, more or less constant, the prisoners confined in the penitentiaries and jails are for the most part kept in enforced idleness. The demands of public institutions for labor, over and above what can be done by their own inmates, are not large enough to afford constant employment for all the prisoners in all the penal institutions of the state; and the constitution has cut off every other resource for prison labor. Unless some new form of labor for public account shall be devised by the legislature, a large percentage of the prisoners within the state must remain in idleness.

The employment of convicts at agriculture has been strongly advocated. In the most southern states of the Union, such work could perhaps be carried on throughout the year, but in the northern states it would not furnish employment during the winter months. Moreover, under the restriction of the New York constitution, the crops raised (being the product, or at least the profits, of convict labor) could not be sold in the general market; only such crops could be cultivated as could be used in public institutions; for example, corn, grain, potatoes, etc. The cultivation of garden vegetables would have to be limited, for the most part, to those supplied to institutions nearby. A New England farmer, with the help of a single hired man, will till a farm of a hundred acres. It is manifest that to employ a thousand or even a hundred convicts at constant farm labor an immense tract of land would be required with a large force of guards, and the product might easily be made too large to supply the available demand. Under the limitations imposed by the New York constitution, but a small fraction of the total number of convicts within the state could be profitably employed in agriculture.

Statutes have been passed authorizing the employment of convicts in improving the public highways, and this form of labor has received a good deal of popular advocacy. Generally, it has not met the approval of prison reformers. To make a public exhibition of convicts is not conducive to their reformation. Even the admission of the public to the prisons as visitors has been proved to have a disturbing and injurious effect on the discipline and morale of the prisons. The reformation of the convicts is best promoted by their strict seclusion from the outside world, so that the reformative influences, which are designed to suppress old associations, ideas and motives, and to awaken new ideals and hopes, may be allowed to operate without interruption and to gain an engrossing power in the convict's life. Convicts working in the public highways are a public spectacle. They are exposed to the jeers and comments, or at least to the frowning stare, of every passer-by; they are constantly reminded that they are objects of public abhorrence and regarded as public enemies. All this is calculated to keep alive in the breast of the convict a sense of his degradation and to arouse a spirit of defiance; if every man's hand is against him, his hand shall be against every man.

The same difficulty in providing a sufficiency of labor in the prisons that is now experienced in New York would be met by every other state adopting the New York system. Some new forms of prison labor which shall satisfy on the one hand the requirements of a reformatory system and on the other the economic demand that the prisoners earn the cost of their support, are still awaiting discovery and development. In the meantime, the problems of prison labor remain unsolved in the United States.

The contest against crime in this country is carried on under some difficulties that are peculiar to the United States. The wide extent of the country covered with a net-work of railways affords the criminal unusual facilities for rapid escape and concealment. There is no registration of the population here (like the *casier judiciaire* in France), nor passport system between states; every person has absolutely unhampered freedom of movement from any point in the United States to its remotest corner. The people of this country are largely of migratory habit, frequently changing their residence from one state or locality to another. It follows that less interest and curiosity are directed toward a stranger or even a neighbor here than in communities more stationary. It will be remembered that when William M. Tweed, under indictment for peculation and fraud in looting the treasury of the city of New York, escaped from the officers who had arrested him, he crossed the Hudson River into the state of New Jersey. There he remained in security for months, actually within sight of the city of New York, while the keenest detectives were scouring land and sea and following every clue in their fruitless search for him.

The difficulty of detection and capture is further enhanced by the large number of foreigners (a million or more per year) immigrating to the United States and adding to the population strange faces, many of which to our unaccustomed eyes look just alike. There arises a special need in this country for ready and effective means of identifying persons accused of crime. Both the Bertillon and the finger print systems of identification are in use in the United States, one or both of these systems having lately been adopted by state authority, and used to a limited extent, in nearly three-quarters of the states of the Union. The state of New York has established a central bureau at Albany where records of identification are received from all the penal institutions of the state, and where the collection amounted in 1908 to over 70,000 individual Bertillon records and 6000 finger print records. A central bureau of criminal identification under federal authority is maintained at the United States prison at Fort Leavenworth, Kansas, where records taken under both systems are received from all penal institutions and police departments, state as well as federal, throughout the Union. The use of identification systems is being rapidly extended, with the prospect that in a few years it will be universally enforced in all the leading cities and penal institutions in the country. The time is probably not far distant when the central bureau at Fort Leavenworth will furnish the means of identifying most of the habitual criminals and recidivists within the United States.

Another source of difficulty, more serious than any other, in the detection and apprehension of criminals, arises from the territorial limit of state jurisdiction. A warrant of arrest issued from a state court in New York, cannot be executed across the line in Connecticut or New Jersey. The federal constitution, it is true, provides that "a person charged, in any state, with treason, felony or other crime, who shall flee from justice and be found in another state, shall, on demand of the executive authority of the state from which he fled, be delivered up, to be removed to the state having jurisdiction of the crime." But the preparation of the papers necessary to obtain such extradition consumes time, when hot haste is sometimes demanded to catch the fugitive. Suppose a crime committed in New York and the New York detectives in pursuit of the escaping criminal have located him in Chicago. He can be arrested in Chicago only by an officer having authority under the laws of Illinois. It can hardly be expected that the Chicago police will exert quite as much alertness, skill and vigilance in the detection and capture of a fugitive from New York as in catching an offender who has committed a crime in their own precinct. For the latter crime they are in a degree responsible and their reputation as well as their duty demands that they must find and arrest the culprit; it is their first and special business to protect their own precinct from crime and there is crime enough in Chicago to engross all their energy. It follows, naturally, that when the offender has once effected his escape into another state his chances for slipping through the meshes of the law are largely increased. It is more difficult to find him and far more difficult, when he is found, to accomplish his actual seizure before he can again disappear.

Our criminal jurisprudence requires that every criminal trial must be held within the state where the crime was committed. One exception is in the case of larceny; where a person has in one state stolen goods which he has carried into another state, he can if arrested there be brought to trial in the latter state. But, by the general rule, the detection and punishment of crime devolve upon the state where the crime was committed, although that state has no power to pursue and apprehend the offender if he has escaped into another state. The states are thus unfortunately handicapped in contending against crime, but, under our constitutional system of state sovereignty, the difficulty appears to be inevitable.

The collection and compilation of criminal statistics in the United States are extremely imperfect. Many of the states have laws requiring the transmission by local courts and officers to a central state office of a record of the number of arrests and convictions; but these laws are loosely observed and the records thus obtained are fragmentary and unreliable. There is lack of uniformity in the statistical systems of the several states, making difficult any attempt to gather together and to tabulate and compare the records of all the states. The only statistics regarding crime that embrace the whole country are those taken by federal authority and appearing in the decennial census of the United States. But no census prior to 1904 went further than to enumerate and classify the prisoners actually serving under sentence in all the prisons in the United States on the 30th day of June of the census year. In 1904, the additional feature was introduced of enumerating all the commitments and sentences for the calendar year 1904. It is a comparatively easy task to count the prisoners in all the prisons on a given day; but it is quite a different task to ascertain the number of commitments and sentences for a period of twelve months. Owing to the immense number of courts, especially those of inferior jurisdiction, within the United States, and the imperfection of their records, it is hardly possible to accomplish the latter task with accuracy; nothing more than a result approximately correct can be expected.

With regard to the vital question, Is crime increasing? it is doubtful whether it is practicable to gather any statistics that will yield an answer. The confident assertion that crime is increasing is frequently made, and in its attempted support appeal is made to the statistics of crime. It is claimed, on the other hand, that a careful analysis of the statistics fails to sustain the assertion. The difficulty is that all official criminal statistics are necessarily confined to those instances of crime that come before the courts or for which arrests are made. If these instances increase in number, the fact may be owing to an increase in crime or it may be the result of greater vigilance and success on the part of the police in making arrests. Indeed, it may be accounted for by numberless causes other than the inferred increase of crime.

For the cases of crime that come before the courts are but a fraction, and doubtless a minor fraction, of the total number of crimes committed. There are countless crimes, the perpetrators of which escape detection: secret crimes, the existence of which is unknown or is perhaps discovered by accident years afterward; crimes, the victims of which fail to bring them to the knowledge of the public authorities, from fear of evil consequences to themselves, or because they shrink from the publicity of prosecution, or because the offender is a near relative whose exposure would disgrace the victim's family, or because of pity for the offender professing penitence, or pity for the offender's family. All these crimes, the specification of which might be indefinitely extended, enter into the volume of crime, but do not and cannot appear in official statistics of crime. There is no possible means of determining the ratio these unpublished crimes bear to the statistical crimes, or whether there is any fixed relation in amount or number between the two classes of crime. If one of the classes increases, it affords no evidence that the other class is also increasing; it may well be that as one increases the other decreases. Both classes together make up the volume of crime; and whether this total volume is increasing or not can never be determined by any statistical measurement of a minor part of the volume, without any possible knowledge of the relation that part bears to the residue.

The criminal law is only one of the instrumentalities that war against crime; there are other forces, educational, philanthropic, religious, that are vastly more effective. Whether crime is increasing or diminishing is a problem that can receive no mathematical or demonstrative solution; the best approach to a solution is by way of comparison between successive ages or periods of time. If we go back several centuries, we cannot fail to perceive that crime was then, to an immense degree, more prevalent and more brutal than it is now. Nothing is more obvious in the historical development of civilization than its humanizing influence on society; by nurturing the sense of justice, respect for law, self-restraint and self-respect, abhorrence of violence and of crime, it has effected a moral transformation in popular sentiment and character. "The mills of the gods grind slowly." But, there is a leaven in Christian civilization that is ever active with a divine potency, irresistible as the flight of time.

56

CHAPTER IV

THE PUNITIVE SYSTEM OF CRIMINAL LAW

THE origin and the early history of the criminal law in the Anglo-Saxon race are not altogether lost in obscurity. Originally, crime appears to have been regarded only as a wrong done to the individual victim, and he was deemed its rightful avenger. The repression of crime was left in large measure to the natural passion of the sufferer for revenge and, when a crime was committed, it was the right (perhaps the duty) of the individual whom the crime had injured and his next of kin to pursue the offender and to inflict summary vengeance upon him. The law sought to regulate the exercise of private vengeance by limiting it within reasonable bounds, by establishing cities of refuge, and by other measures designed to restrain its unbridled indulgence. In that turbulent age, however, all these restraints were powerless to prevent blood-feuds and the increasing prevalence of private war. The license of individual vengeance was incompatible with public order and became intolerable; it was from necessity abrogated and its exercise was declared illegal. But the law could not repeal or weaken the universal sentiment of the time, which not only demanded vengeance upon the criminal but could not even conceive of any method of repressing crime except by putting the criminal to death or subjecting him to vindictive punishment.

The infliction of vengeance, forbidden to the individual, was simply transferred to the body politic; for the private avenger was substituted the public avenger. The change was logically effected through the evolution of a political theory defining the function of the governing power in its relation to crime. This was the theory: that crime was a public, more than a private wrong, doing greater injury to the public than to the individual; that the state, representing all its subjects and the whole people, was thus the supreme sufferer from crime; and, consequently, that the state and not the individual victim, was the rightful avenger of crime. The state, with its unrestrained power, proved an even more terrible and relentless avenger than the individual had been. The most vindictive

57

punishments and the cruelest tortures that malignant ingenuity could devise were practiced under the sanction of law and in the name of justice.

From the earliest time, the attempt was made to graduate the severity of the punishment to the enormity of the offense. Laws were made defining the various crimes, assuming to admeasure their comparative degrees of guilt, and assigning to each crime its proportionate amount of punishment. These laws were always animated by the primitive motive of vengeance; they had the single aim to balance punishment and guilt and to inflict on the criminal an amount of suffering or damage that should be commensurate with the guilt of his crime. Compensatory retribution, measuring guilt in terms of pain, was the visionary ideal of the law and its only end.

The refining influences of Christian civilization have tempered the cruelty of previous ages in the practical administration of the criminal law. Tortures have long disappeared and humane efforts have been made to improve the sanitation and the morale of the prisons, but the motives and principles which governed the development of our criminal law centuries ago have remained unchanged down to the present generation. The modern penal codes are *fundamentally* exact reproductions of those of the middle ages. True, the modern codes contain different definitions of different crimes and prescribe different punishments; but, like the ancient codes, they are composed of definitions of crimes and allotments of punishment to each crime; like the ancient codes, they assume to admeasure the guilt of crimes and to weigh and assort them according to defined degrees, and all for the purpose of assigning to each offense an amount of punishment that shall be exactly apportioned to the measure of guilt in the offender. Not only in form but in purpose and principle the modern codes are duplicates of the ancient ones. In both alike, the sole aim in dealing with the criminal is the infliction of retributive pain and suffering which having been endured shall serve to atone for the crime and to be imputed to him for righteousness, restoring him to freedom as if he had never committed a crime; in both codes alike, the court is required at the trial to probe the soul of the prisoner, —measure the length, breadth and depth of its guiltiness and the equivalent amount of atoning punishment,—and then and there pronounce the mathematical sentence.

It is possible that the system just described may be as creditable a product as could be expected from the crude age which originated it. Perhaps it has equal merit with the grotesque systems of philosophy, filled with wild vagaries, of which the medieval schoolmen were the authors. But it is a wonderful fact that this ancient system of criminal law, based upon assumptions that are obviously false and upon ideals that are not only impracticable and valueless but clearly impossible of attainment, is still accepted in the present enlightened age and still has wide prevalence as a working system among progressive nations throughout the world. The fact itself, however, raises a strong presumption in favor of the system, and in assailing the system it is freely recognized that the assailant bears the entire burden of proof.

The modern (as well as the ancient) penal codes *assume* that crimes are susceptible of general definitions that can be practically applied to concrete instances. They *assume* that each defined crime involves an equal or uniform amount of guilt or criminality in the offender in every case whenever and wherever that crime may be committed. They *assume* that whenever two persons are convicted of committing an assault (for example) under circumstances (or, rather, under such circumstances as are admissible in evidence) which fulfill all the terms and conditions of its definition, both persons are equally guilty and should receive the same punishment. They *assume* that the amount of an offender's guilt can be estimated from the particular crime which he is proved to have committed. They assume the possibility of admeasuring the degree or amount of criminality in an offender and of expressing it in terms of years of imprisonment. They assume the possibility of weighing and of expressing the relative amounts of criminality in widely different crimes (assault and larceny, for example). They assume that sentences of imprisonment for the same number of years pronounced upon several offenders inflict the same or an equal punishment upon each.

Let us pause here to examine the tenability of these various assumptions, all of which are fundamental in the penal codes.

Definitions are necessarily generic and academic; every crime actually committed is special and individual. Crimes of the same name have infinite variations arising from outward circumstances, which are never an exact reproduction of a previous instance, and variations arising far more from inward, subjective, conditions in the mind and character of the culprit. All these variations are vital elements in any attempted computation of the offender's guilt, and most of them are necessarily excluded from any general definition. Consider a few of these vital elements of guilt which surround every criminal trial and yet are seldom matters of evidence or brought at all within the cognizance of the court.   There may be causes of provocation which have operated on the mind of the offender with cumulative force during a long series of years until they culminated in a sudden frenzy of rage; there may be misunderstandings, misapprehensions, mistakes regarding facts, under which the apparent crime was committed; indeed, there is an infinite variety of conceivable facts, aggravating or palliating a crime, which are wholly inadmissible in evidence and are known only to Omniscience, and yet they may be the essential, really vital, factors for any true estimate of guilt. Still more inaccessible are the subjective elements existing in the character of the person accused, without a knowledge of which any computation of guilt is impossible; there are questions of hereditary tendencies, of parental training, of environment, of natural strength or weakness of will and of conscience, of education, of degrees of intelligence or ignorance, of experience, of natural dullness or brightness of mind, of constitutional force or sluggishness of physical passions and appetites.   With these recondite, yet determining, factors beyond the possibility of human ken, the effort to gauge the amount of guilt in any crime is one that the Supreme Intelligence alone can attempt.   No more chimerical and hopeless enterprise has ever been undertaken by the human mind than to construct a code which shall with accuracy and justice define all crimes and tabulate them with their respective degrees of guiltiness.

The assumption of the codes that the nature of the crime committed affords an index to the degree of criminality in the offender, and that the greater the enormity of the crime, the greater is the degree of guiltiness in the person who commits it, is contradicted by experience.   It is the testimony of those who have had large experience in the charge and management of prisons that the crime for which a prisoner has been convicted affords no index of his character. It is often found that those convicted of grave felonies are more amenable to reformative influence than some who are sentenced for minor misdemeanors.   A petty thief, for instance, may prove more obdurate and vicious, more irreclaimable in his wickedness, than some of those who have committed most flagrant crimes.

So, the assumption that the same sentence inflicts the same punishment, when pronounced upon different persons, is untrue. The effect is governed by individual temperaments.   A hardened offender may serve the sentence with phlegmatic apathy; he may have served many similar sentences before.   A prisoner of more sensitive temperament, perhaps a novice, who has seen better days and has not yet lost all pride and self-respect, is overwhelmed with a sense of shame at the disgrace of imprisonment, and its hardships and ignominies bear upon him with the force of torture.

Another feature of the punitive system which perhaps is practically its most dangerous feature, is its doctrine of atonement, holding that when a convict has served out the term of his sentence he has atoned for his crime and is entitled to immediate release. This is supposed to be the logical corollary of retributive punishment. The idea may possibly be traced from the Saxon law which established an elaborate scale of money fines for various crimes; these fines were the purchase price, or compensatory retribution, to be paid by the offender for committing the crime and, when the fines were fully paid, the offender was of course absolved and became exempt from further prosecution. In the same manner, when imprisonment came to be the general form of punishment it was regarded as a penalty imposed, and when the culprit had served his term he had fully paid the price charged by the state for his particular crime and had satisfied all the demands of justice.

Perhaps there is some conflict here with the modern conception of atonement. Suffering endured voluntarily, when accompanied with penitence and restitution, may be accepted as an atonement for a crime. But does not the atoning virtue of the suffering consist in its voluntary and repentant character? How can suffering, inflicted by compulsion and borne with unrepentant defiance, atone for crime or serve to purge the offender of his crime?

However this may be, the dogma in effect produces the most pernicious results. It causes the immediate discharge of the convict upon the expiration of his allotted term of imprisonment, without the slightest regard to his fitness for freedom. It matters not how hardened or vicious the known character of the prisoner may be; he may even openly declare his fixed purpose to return to the life of crime; the state, by reason of this absurd theory of atonement, refuses to exercise any further constraint and turns the convict loose, knowing that he goes forth to be the scourge of the community. Was adherence by the government to a false academic dogma ever carried out to its extreme relentless conclusions with results so damaging to the people and with such criminal disregard of the plainest duty of protection owed by the state to its subjects?

The sole aim of the punitive system as embodied in the penal codes was to punish criminals and to so apportion the punishment to desert as to make it in every case exactly and evenly retributive. But it was perceived long ago that this attempt to realize the conception of ideal justice could not possibly succeed if a uniform amount of punishment was attached to each defined crime. It was perfectly obvious that separate crimes, included under the same definition but committed by different persons under different circumstances, involved different degrees of guilt and hence deserved different amounts of punishment. In other words, it became clearly apparent that perfect retributive justice was absolutely unattainable by any possible penal code. Instead of abandoning the ideal, however, the codes were given a measure of elasticity. The admeasurements of guilt and of corresponding punishment were made approximate only, and the codes, instead of allotting an exact punishment, to each crime, used such expressions as (for example) "imprisonment for not less than five nor more than ten years" or "not exceeding twenty years." This throws upon the judge conducting the trial the real burden of computing the degree of the prisoner's guilt within the limits imposed by the code. The discriminations which the legislature could not possibly make are shifted to the presiding judge.

It is a cruel responsibility cast upon the judge, who is as powerless as the legislature to arrive at a just solution of the problem—to measure and weigh the guilt that rests on the soul of a fellow creature. The determining elements of that problem consist in facts and influences that have operated ever since, and even before, the birth of the prisoner in moulding his character and purposes; in circumstances that are no part of the *res gestae* attending the crime; in thoughts and intents of the heart that are locked up in the prisoner's breast. All these elements are unknown to the judge, and even many of those that may be accessible are rigidly excluded from evidence because not immediately and directly connected with the crime. What possible course is open to the judge, who must decide this momentous problem of human guilt, solvable only by the Almighty? He must be governed by the impression created by the prisoner's appearance and bearing and such meagre facts as are included in the testimony, throwing, or seeming to throw, a gleam of disclosure upon the prisoner's hidden character and purposes. Upon such superficial and undecisive incidents, and upon the force with which they happen to strike the judicial mind, hangs the amount of punishment meted out to the prisoner. The most conscientious judge cannot possibly do otherwise than render a hap-hazard sentence—it may be five years, it may be twenty years. Five years for one prisoner, twenty years for another who is guilty of a similar crime; and the one who receives the longer sentence will (rightly or wrongly) have a rankling sense of injustice which will embitter all his subsequent life.

This burden of decision cast upon the judge involves another injurious consequence. The judge has an individual character and temperament, as well as the prisoner. One judge has a constitutional inclination toward lenity, a deep pity for human frailty, broad sympathy and charity; another is a severe and relentless judge of character, moved by an abhorrence of crime that is little tempered with mercy. Both judges may be animated by the same conscientious aim to act justly, and yet it is certain that the same prisoner will receive, if tried before one of them, a sentence of not more than five years and, if tried before the other, a sentence of not less than ten years. Add to this discrepancy the wide variation in the penalties for the same crime in the codes of the different states (as shown in the preceding chapter), and it is evident that there is no standard, no consensus of opinion, by which it is possible to make any practical approach toward equality in punitive sentences.

The ideal of equal and exact justice aimed at by the penal codes is unattainable; even partial or approximate justice the codes can never attain. The pretence of administering justice, while the real results are known to be grossly unjust, casts discredit and derision on the penal codes; the glaring uncertainty and inequality in the distribution of punishments make the name of legal justice a mockery. And thus the moral effect which the criminal law ought to have upon the public mind, by appealing to the sense of righteousness, is sadly impaired and almost destroyed.

This arraignment of the penal codes and the punitive system they embody is based upon facts that are universally known, and yet these codes and their system still retain their hold over a large part of the civilized world. Such is the tenacious strength of the human aspiration for justice, an unattainable ideal!

The just test of any institution is in its practical working and the effects it accomplishes. Has the punitive system served to repress or diminish crime? In the civilizing processes of the ages, crime has certainly decreased and there is reason to believe that it is still decreasing. There are innumerable forces, educational, philanthropic, Christian forces, that are successfully warring against crime. Is the punitive system of criminal law one of these beneficent forces?

Reference to a single fact will perhaps be accepted as a satisfactory answer to this question. Most of the convicts in the United

States who have served the term of their sentence in state prisons or penitentiaries, conducted as these prisons were a century ago, and as most of them are now conducted, on the punitive plan, return to a life of crime after their release. This is not true of all these convicts. The fact that some of them live within the law after their discharge may be explained, it is thought, chiefly by the circumstance that the treatment in the punitive prisons has one, and only one, reformative feature; that is, hard labor. Where a prisoner is kept steadily employed at industrial work, day after day and year after year, he acquires, perforce, the *habit* of labor. This habit thus formed has enough virtue in itself in some cases to sustain the discharged convict in a life of honest industry. What actual percentage of these convicts abstain from crime after release is a matter of estimate, but the highest claim made by the prison wardens in this behalf is twenty-five per cent. This figure suggests a simple computation. The total number of convicts now confined in the punitive, non-reformative prisons in the United States is approximately 80,000. The average term of sentence served is about four years, giving an annual discharge of 20,000. Assuming, as claimed, that one-quarter of these live a law-abiding life, the remaining 15,000 resume the life of crime. This 15,000 includes the most confirmed and desperate criminals in the United States; they go out from the prisons, acknowledged experts in crime, to become a terror to the community. Every year the prisons in the United States discharge upon the country this vast army of criminals, hardened and made more desperate by their prison life, to replenish and to lead the criminal class. And all this is done by reason of a blind subservience to the ancient and absurd theory that these ex-convicts have atoned for their crimes. Of all the agencies and influences that tend to the increase of crime in the United States, it is safe to declare that the penal codes and the punitive system of the criminal law, inheritances from the middle ages, are the most potent and insidious

CHAPTER V

THE INDETERMINATE SENTENCE

AMONG the false assumptions involved in the penal codes the primal assumption, underlying all the others, is that which defines the function of the state in relation to crime Originally, the state, we have seen, became the "avenger of crime." That conception, somewhat modified, is still embodied in the codes. They assume that the whole duty of the state with reference to the criminal is discharged by the infliction of retributive punishment. They aim at an ideal, but unattainable, *justice* in the treatment of the prisoner, and nothing more.

This is a very superficial and false view of the functions of the state. The state exists for the *protection* of the people. The state does not properly interfere with the operation of natural laws governing the development and the activities of the people, until something arises which obstructs their free operation and becomes, or threatens to be, harmful to the public weal. The aim of all rightful legislation is protection of the public against injury, against whatever is a menace to progress, liberty, peace. Crime is one of these injurious factors in the common life against which, as against contagious disease and homicidal insanity, it is the duty of the state to protect the people. The rightful object of all criminal law is public defence against crime. The state confines a patient having a contagious disease in a hospital, a violent lunatic in an asylum, a criminal in a prison; in each case it is dangerous to the community to allow the person confined to be at large, and the action of the state, in each case alike, is justified by its duty of securing the public safety.

These two distinct conceptions of the relation of the state to crime lead to results that are wide apart. The view embodied in the penal codes lays stress upon the treatment of the criminal; its keynote is retributive punishment; its ideal is to do exact justice to the criminal and, to attain this end, the effort is made to admeasure guilt and apportion punishment; but while effort is thus concentrated on the criminal, the codes, with their theory of atonement, lose sight of the duty of the state toward the people.

On the other hand, the broader and correct view of the functions of the state lays controlling stress upon the defence of the public against crime; public protection is its key-note, and it demands that the treatment of the criminal shall be subordinated, and if possible made conducive, to that main end. Under this latter view, the degree of the prisoner's guilt and even the exact academic definition of his crime become mere speculative and wholly immaterial questions. The fact that he has committed a crime, rendering it incompatible with public safety that he should be at large, makes it the duty of the state not only to put him in prison but to keep him in prison until it becomes consistent with public safety to set him free. But how long then shall the imprisonment last? The plain and convincing answer is—until the prisoner becomes fitted for freedom.

It is for the obvious interest of the convict, and of the public as well, that he should be transformed in character and be fitted to live an honest and law-abiding life, and that this result should be accomplished in the shortest possible time. But can this result be accomplished at all, and how can it be accomplished? Is this result as visionary and unattainable as the ancient ideal of retributive justice has proved to be? The punitive system, by the experience of centuries, has demonstrated that mere imprisonment has of itself no reformative influence; on the contrary, the association and the stern discipline in the punitive prison have generally produced a hardening and demoralizing effect. That the convict should reform himself, without any uplifting aid, without any outward source of encouragement and hope, is well nigh impossible. How, then, can the prison life fit him for freedom?

The modern system of reformatory treatment, that may be said to owe its origin to the genius of Z. R. Brockway, the founder and for many years the superintendent of the state reformatory at Elmira, New York, has been adopted and is now administered in a considerable number of prisons in the most progressive states of the Union. The various agencies and methods which have been scientifically developed by experiment and are embodied in this system of training and discipline, are rather subjects of practical administration than of legislation, and are therefore outside the scope of the present writing. It is sufficient to state here, in a summary way, the results accomplished. The reformatory system has been applied, until very recently, only to the treatment of first offenders and, generally, to those under thirty years of age. Its application is now being extended, tentatively, to state prisons, which have heretofore been conducted under the punitive plan, and it is believed that the system can be successfully adapted to all prisons and to all prisoners convicted of crime.

As to the results obtained by this reformatory system, it must be remembered that the danger of a relapse into crime is most acute in the months immediately following the convict's release from prison. The sudden removal of restraint is apt to cause a reaction; the difficulty that the convict experiences in readjusting himself to the changed conditions of freedom, and the temptation, arising from that very difficulty, to return to his old mode of life, press hardest upon him at the beginning. It is the first step that costs. If he exhibits sufficient strength of purpose to stand firm against the shock of the first rebound; if, at the end of six months, he has become established in industrial occupation, has avoided evil associations and is determined to live honestly; has he not endured the severest test? Is it an unfair presumption that he has really entered upon a new life and that he will hereafter retain both the purpose and the ability to abstain from crime? The men from the Elmira Reformatory have been subjected to this crucial test and its statistics show that eighty per cent of them have stood the test successfully. This reformatory system of prison treatment has now become firmly established as an institution in the United States, and present tendencies indicate that it will ultimately gain universal prevalence throughout the country.

The length of time required by such reformatory treatment to fit a convict for freedom can be determined only by actual trial in every case; it is purely a question of individual character and temperament, and bears no relation to the crime committed. Manifestly it cannot be measured by a term fixed in advance. The convict resists and is naturally hostile to reforming influences; until he yields himself to them and co-operates with them, no beneficent result can be attained. But if he is confined under a definite sentence for a fixed term, the knowledge that he will be absolutely entitled to his discharge in any event at the end of the term, encourages him to maintain an attitude of defiant resistance to all reforming influences. The definite sentence is, therefore, distinctly adverse to reformation; adverse to every effort toward fitting the convict for freedom.

To meet the demands of a reformatory system and to obviate the evils of the punitive system, the indeterminate sentence has been devised. By this, the person convicted of crime is to be sentenced to imprisonment for no specified term, but to remain in confinement and under reformative treatment until he becomes fit for freedom.

This form of sentence logically involves not only the reformatory system with all its approved appliances and methods for developing in the prisoner correct principles and habits, but also in every case constant observation and a minute personal record, together with applied tests, showing the steps toward progress and toward relapse. In this way, the career of each convict, the development of his character and purposes, his power of self-control, will become so far revealed to the officers of the prison and to the Board of Parole that the question whether he has attained fitness for freedom can be determined with a prognosis not less reliable and confident than that with which (for example) a lunatic is declared to have regained his sanity. The prisoner, knowing that his discharge is dependent on his own exertions, will be impelled by the longing for liberty (the most effective of all possible incentives) to surrender himself to the uplifting influences that surround him. And the discharge when earned by the prisoner is a conditional one; he goes at once to a place where employment has been secured for him, and the state extends its protecting care and supervision over him through a period of parole. During this period (usually six months or a year) he is required to render monthly reports made by himself and his employer showing the amount of his earnings and the character of his work. At the end of this period, if he has demonstrated his ability and purpose to lead an honest life of self-support, he receives an absolute discharge. But if, during the period of parole, he commits a crime or falls into evil ways or among bad associations, he is re-arrested and returned to the reformatory for further treatment.

The theory of the indeterminate sentence seems to have attained at last the ideal of justice, after which the criminal law has for ages been vainly striving. Justice to the people, by protection against crime; and to the criminal, not only justice but mercy in the form of Christian beneficence. Imprisonment for a fixed term under the old punitive system yields only temporary protection to society, lasting until the expiration of the term, when the original danger is revived in an aggravated form. The indeterminate sentence makes the protection permanent. Reformation of the convict, therefore, becomes the highest and ultimate aim of imprisonment, for nothing but reformation or continued imprisonment can absolutely secure the public against his depredations.

The indeterminate sentence reverses the attitude of the state toward the criminal and hence tends to reverse the attitude of the criminal toward the state. Under the punitive system, the convict regards the state defiantly as an avenging fury, inflicting upon him pain and suffering and finally casting him out with threatenings for the future. Under the reformatory system, the idea of punishment is kept in the background and the state presents itself to the convict as a beneficent power aiming to effect his rehabilitation and to aid him in becoming worthy of freedom.

The indeterminate sentence is not applicable to all crimes. It ought not to be applied to those gravest crimes, denominated capital crimes, which do irremediable and deadly harm. For the decision that a convict is fitted for release, like the decision that a lunatic has recovered sanity, may be quite correct at the time when rendered, but in neither case is it possible to guarantee that there will be no relapse in the future. The most that can be affirmed regarding the permanence of the cure in any case is that there will *probably* be no recurrence of the malady. This probability does not over-balance the mere possibility that one who has once committed a deadly crime may be capable of repeating it; the danger to the public is too great to justify the risk of releasing him.

On the other hand, for a wholly different reason, there may be a question whether the indeterminate sentence can justly be applied to all the minor crimes and petty misdemeanors. The reformatory treatment has proved effective upon the great majority of the convicts subjected to it, and its success appears to bear little relation to the gravity of the crimes they have committed. But some convicts have always proved unresponsive to reformative influence and are apparently incorrigible by any form of human instrumentality yet discovered. If all such convicts without distinction were held under the indeterminate sentence, they would be kept in confinement during life. The logical principle of this sentence is, no release, except for those who are fit for freedom; and if the original offense was such that public protection justified the imprisonment of the offender, the same reason demands the continuance of the imprisonment until the prisoner has undergone such a change of character as gives reasonable promise that if set free he will not again commit crime. If the crime committed is one that imports serious danger to the community, the logic of the indeterminate sentence is unanswerable. There is no justification to the state in turning loose upon the people a felon who has proved impervious to all reforming influences and agencies and who is sure to resume his previous life of depredation and crime until he is again caught and imprisoned. Such a convict can complain of no injustice to himself if he is held in permanent confinement, and in no other way can the public be effectively protected.

But in the case of petty misdemeanors, the situation presents a different phase and is more difficult of solution. These offenses import, not serious danger but rather inconvenience and annoyance to the public. If the offender is committed under the indeterminate sentence, he is quite as likely as a felon is to resist reformatory treatment, and he may consequently be held in prison during his lifetime. Here, again, the logic of the indeterminate sentence is inexorable. The people are entitled to protection against minor, as well as graver, crimes; the laws must be enforced; it is an absurdity to put a misdemeanant in prison and then, after a brief term, to release him, with the assurance that he will immediately commit the same, or a more flagrant, offense. Short sentences often repeated for petty offenses serve no useful purpose and are distinctly injurious.

On the other hand, it is a most serious matter to deprive a human being of liberty by a life-long imprisonment; only urgent necessity justifies the state in resorting to so extreme a measure. Take the crime of "drunkenness and disorderly conduct;" it is the most common offense brought before the inferior courts and the most difficult one to dispose of satisfactorily. If habitual drunkenness is a disease, it should be treated as such; the drunkard should be committed to a retreat as a patient for medical treatment until cured. If the disease proves incurable or the habit unconquerable, why should it seem more unjust to confine the patient for life than to keep an incurable lunatic in an asylum for life? With this, as with many other misdemeanors, there is the practical difficulty of procuring any verdict of guilty from a jury, if such verdict entails the possibility of a virtual life sentence against the prisoner. Moreover, there is the serious question whether these minor offenses *do* constitute such a menace and danger to the community as to justify the state in resorting to a remedy so drastic and extreme as a condemnation of the offender to what may be life imprisonment. It may be that the reformatory system of treatment (which is now in a stage largely experimental in this country) will be so perfected in the future that it may become expedient and just to bring all crimes under an absolutely indeterminate sentence.

Imprisonment, however, is not always the best, or even a desirable, form of treatment for habitual inebriety. Unless the confinement, with enforced abstinence, is continued for a sufficiently long period to overcome the passion for strong drink, imprisonment will hardly exert any curative effect, while its deterrent influence is almost negligible. There are instances, as already stated, where medical treatment in a sanitarium or inebriate asylum presents the hope of effecting a cure. In many other cases, not so inveterate, a suspension of sentence committing the offender to the charge of a probation officer has produced good results. In Chicago and St. Louis this latter course has been adopted with the condition that the culprit sign a pledge of total abstinence for one year, and the effect of the system in the two cities is favorably reported.

The chief difficulty in applying the indeterminate sentence to minor offenses consists in the fact that in an obdurate case it may be a life sentence. This difficulty disappears when the sentence is qualified by imposing a maximum limit to the possible duration of the imprisonment; and if the maximum limit is made large enough, the indeterminate sentence thus limited seems the best possible treatment for misdemeanors and minor offenses generally. It does away with the evil of short, repeated sentences, and goes as far as public sentiment at the present time will approve.

The indeterminate sentence has been received by the people with such favor that it is now incorporated, in modified forms, in the criminal jurisprudence of many states of the Union. In all these states, however, it is qualified by confining its operation between a minimum and a maximum limit. Although it is hard to regard such limitation as logically defensible, there is much to be said in favor of it from a practical point of view.

The plan of the indeterminate sentence had its origin here within the present generation; it was not only new to the people but its principle was in conflict with those fundamental conceptions of retributive punishment upon which the whole criminal law had rested from time immemorial. The inherited idea, that justice demands that the duration of the imprisonment be governed by the gravity of the offense, was so firmly implanted in the public mind that it is difficult to eradicate it. It will still require time to educate public opinion to full acceptance of the belief that the true aim of imprisonment is not to inflict retributive suffering upon the prisoner, but to make him fit for freedom; that the imprisonment should continue until that aim is accomplished, no matter now long it may take, and no matter what the prisoner's crime may have been; that, in perfect analogy to a hospital or an insane asylum, a prison is only a sanitarium where every inmate must be retained and treated until he is cured and can safely be discharged. The indeterminate sentence without limits cannot be adopted, in fact, until these beliefs have supplanted the ancient ones and have become thoroughly grounded in the public mind. Moreover, the indeterminate sentence presupposes an effective reformatory system of treatment, with tests and means of accurately judging results accomplished in each individual case. Until all these have been developed by experiment to a high degree of scientific efficiency, it is perhaps quite as well that the maximum limit should be retained.

Graver objections have been made to the minimum, than to the maximum, limit. The prisoner is informed at the outset that it is possible for him to earn his discharge within the minimum term, say two years. He and his friends look forward to the expiration of the two years as the date when he will be set free, very much as if he had received a definite sentence for two years. This anticipation (it is said by prison authorities) relaxes his efforts and goes far to neutralize the virtue of the indeterminate feature of the sentence; and when the two years have elapsed and the prisoner's record does not justify his release, he is apt to regard his further detention with a sense of injustice as if it were a new sentence or an extension of his original sentence.

The principle of the indeterminate sentence so appeals to the sense of justice, and the attachment to it of a maximum limit so disarms the inherited popular prejudice in favor of a fixed sentence, that the danger now threatening the country is, not that this indeterminate form of sentence may be neglected, but that it may be too generally adopted and prematurely applied before the prisons are adapted to receive it. It seems perfectly obvious that the indeterminate sentence is the complement of a reformatory prison system; of a system which not only effects reform, but furnishes tests and evidences of what it has accomplished in each individual case. In disregard of this plain precedent condition, a tendency has become manifest to apply the indeterminate sentence to all prisons indiscriminately. To condemn a convict to imprisonment in a state prison conducted upon the old punitive plan, without any reformative or uplifting agencies, except possibly hard labor,—and nearly all the prisons in the United States are still conducted upon that ancient plan,—and to command him to fit himself for freedom as the condition of his release, is a cruel mockery. The parole boards, moreover, are often composed of men who have no proper understanding of the importance or the nature of their duties; they are apt to pass upon the applications for discharge that are submitted to them, in a hasty and perfunctory manner, with the inevitable result that prisoners are released who are wholly unfitted for freedom and speedily relapse into crime. Both these causes—the administration of the indeterminate sentence in non-reformative prisons and the incompetency of boards of parole—not only serve to impair the usefulness of this form of sentence but tend to bring the sentence itself into disrepute. There is now very serious danger that the value of the indeterminate sentence as a powerful auxiliary to reform may fail of recognition and the sentence fall into discredit, by reason of the improper uses to which it is being subjected.

The validity of the laws establishing the indeterminate sentence has been repeatedly assailed in the courts upon constitutional grounds, but unsuccessfully in every instance except one. The grounds of attack have been that such laws violated the state constitutions in the following particulars: in vesting judicial power in the boards of parole, which are given authority to discharge the convict; in encroaching upon the governor's constitutional power of pardon and vesting such power in the parole board; in depriving the court of all discretion in fixing the term of imprisonment; in depriving the defendant of the right of a Common Law jury trial; and in inflicting a cruel and unusual punishment. (*George v. People*, 167 *Illinois R.* 447; *Miller v. State*, 149 *Indiana R.* 607; *Skelton v. State*, 149 *Indiana R.* 641; *Wilson v. State*, 150 *Indiana R.* 297; *State v. Peters*, 43 *Ohio St. R.* 629; *Commonwealth v. Brown*, 167 *Massachusetts R.* 144; *Conlon's case*, 148 *Massachusetts R.* 168.) The one exceptional instance, mentioned above, in which this form of sentence was held to be unconstitutional, was the case of *People v. Cummings*, decided in the State of Michigan in 1891 (88 *Mich. R.* 249). The decision was rendered nugatory, however, by the prompt action of the people of the state in so amending the constitution of Michigan as to meet the objections upon which the decision rested; and in 1903 a new indeterminate sentence law was enacted in conformity with the new constitution. It has been held in several states that a statute establishing the indeterminate sentence properly applies only to offenses committed after the enactment of the statute, and that if applied to prior offenses it would be an *ex post facto* law. (*Johnson v. People*, 173 *Illinois R.* 131; *Murphy v. Commonwealth*, 172 *Massachusetts R.* 264; *People v. Dane*, 81 *Michigan R.* 36.)

The attack upon the indeterminate sentence law of Illinois was carried to the Supreme Court of the United States upon the claim

73

that the law was repugnant to the 14th amendment of the United States Constitution, which declares that no state shall "deprive any person of life, liberty or property without due process of law." The Supreme Court sustained the constitutionality of the law. (*Dreyer v. Illinois*, 187 *U. S.* 71). This decision rendered in October, 1902, will probably be accepted as having definitively settled the legality of the indeterminate sentence.

The indeterminate sentence, unhampered with either minimum or maximum limits, has never been tested. These limits seriously impair its effectiveness, but the time is not yet ripe for their removal. When the reformatory system of prison training and discipline shall be further perfected (and rapid progress is now making in that direction), and such system shall have become established in all prisons throughout the United States, public opinion may demand the universal adoption and enforcement of the indeterminate sentence in its absolute form. This is not a visionary anticipation. The tendencies of the present are flowing with a strong current in favor of the development and extension of a reformatory prison system; the danger is that the current flows so strongly in favor of the indeterminate sentence that states may adopt it prematurely before the prisons and their officers are fitted to administer it.

If in the fullness of time the conditions shall justify the use of the indeterminate sentence, unlimited and absolute, it is difficult to overestimate its efficacy as an aid to reformation and as a means of protection to the public against crime. It applies to the prisoner the strongest possible incentive to submit himself to the benign influences surrounding him, and by their aid, to work out his own salvation. It opens to him one single and only path to freedom. The release from prison of an unregenerate criminal is a bane to the public, but it is a far greater curse to the criminal himself; enslaved by appetites and passions that are evil, without power of self-control, unable to withstand temptation, he needs the constraint and guidance of a strong arm. To withdraw that constraint by setting him free is to abandon him to evil forces that will drag him to greater depths of crime. There is no more fatal doom for such a criminal than freedom. The indeterminate sentence defends the criminal from his worst enemy, himself, aims to awaken hope, to develop character, to infuse strength, to purify, elevate, re-form the whole man; and thus it embodies the very spirit of the teachings and life of the Savior of men.

CHAPTER VI

CHILDREN'S COURTS AND PROBATION OFFICERS

AMONG the contributions made by the United States toward the development of the science of penology upon practical lines, there are four of signal value and importance. These are (1) the Elmira system of reformatory discipline and training; (2) the indeterminate sentence; (3) children's courts, and (4) the institution of probation, with probation officers. The first of these is the product of prison administration rather than of legislation, and is not therefore included within the scope of the present work. The indeterminate sentence has been treated in the preceding chapter. The two remaining subjects, children's courts and probation, are claimed as American institutions; whether or not one or both of them originated in the United States, in the sense that here they preceded everything of an analogous character found in any other country, they have become so firmly established and so extensively used in the United States that they now constitute very distinctive features of American jurisprudence. The usefulness of both these institutions depends vitally upon the spirit and the methods of their administration; but it is proposed in this concluding chapter, to consider only the *laws* governing their creation and regulation.

At Common Law, the age below which a child was held incapable of committing crime was fixed at seven years; and Blackstone cites a case where a boy eight years old was convicted of arson and hanged. Between the ages of seven and fourteen, a child, though regarded as not incapable of committing a felony, was judged "by the strength of the delinquent's understanding and judgment." But when a child reached the mature age of fourteen, the Common Law held him to the same degree of responsibility as an adult for felonies committed. The rigor of the law might in fact be softened by the humane temper of a judge inclined to mercy, but the Common Law relating to felonies made no distinction of persons among those over fourteen years of age.

It seems almost incredible that these medieval views of childhood, embodied in the Common Law, should find expression in any

75

penal code of the twentieth century. But the provisions of the penal code of the progressive state of New York regarding the criminal responsibility of children are the following:

Sec. 816. A child under the age of seven years is not capable of committing crime.

Sec. 817. A child of the age of seven years and under the age of twelve years, is presumed to be incapable of crime, but the presumption may be removed by proof that he had sufficient capacity to understand the act or neglect charged against him and to know its wrongfulness.

This code is even more rigorous than the Common Law, as it reduces from fourteen to twelve years the limit of age within which a child is presumptively incapable of crime. A child above the age of twelve years stood on the same footing as an adult, inasmuch as the sections above quoted were, until 1894, the only provisions on the subject contained in the code. In 1894, an act was passed providing that when a child under the age of fourteen (since raised to sixteen) was charged with a crime, other than a capital crime, which if committed by an adult would be a felony, the child could be tried as for a misdemeanor. From this exception of a capital crime, it follows that there is nothing in the law of New York at the present day to prevent the conviction and execution of a child eight years old for murder.

Before the enactment of the laws creating children's courts, the judges, upon the trial of children for crime, were often constrained by the mandatory language of the codes. Where the code declares that the commission of such and such an act *by any person* constitutes such a crime and fixes its penalty, and directs that the magistrate before whom the trial is had *shall impose* the penalty prescribed by law, the only question before the court is whether the child has in fact committed the act defined, with knowledge of its wrongfulness. If the evidence has answered that question in the affirmative, the magistrate, however merciful his impulses and however tender the age of the child (provided it is over seven), is apt to regard the code as leaving nothing to his discretion, but imperatively commanding him to impose the penalty it prescribes; and to fear that by failing to do so, in the case of a child just as in the case of an adult, he would himself be guilty of a violation of the law.

There were other matters equally important in which the judge had no power of discretion. The accused child often had to be committed to the common jail while awaiting trial; the law provided no other place of confinement. If convicted and sentenced, the child generally had to be imprisoned in the jail or the penitentiary, in common with old and hardened criminals. In a word, the codes were no respecters of persons; their procedure, their crimes and their punishments, all related simply to "persons"—a child was a person— and the codes practically ignored the existence of any essential difference between a child over seven years of age and an adult.

It was the tardy recognition of the distance that separates the child from the adult that led to the creation of children's courts. Perhaps it would be too much to say that a criminal less than sixteen years of age is an impossibility. There are rare instances of abnormal development which, in the apparent absence or atrophy of the moral sense, rapidly converts a mere child into a prodigy of wickedness and crime; but even in such cases, the cause can generally be traced to an exceptionally vicious environment. But generally the act of a child, which if done by an adult would constitute crime, hardly deserves so severe a name. The child may, and usually does, know that the act is wrong, but he has no adequate realization of its wrongfulness or of the reason why it is wrong; he often lacks the experience and the judgment to discriminate between an act that is merely mischievous and one that is unlawful. A child is essentially imitative and is apt to do what he sees his elders doing, without thinking whether it is right or wrong. The moral sense in a rudimentary form appears very early in life, but its development, together with that of the other reflective faculties, is slower than the development of the emotional nature; during the period of childhood, the imperative of conscience is generally feeble. Hence it is that the primary formation of character is largely the product of the atmosphere and external influences surrounding the child, the conscience and reason not having yet grown strong enough to cope with the environment.

The Common Law methods of dealing with delinquent children as if they were adults are extremely harmful; in the case of adults those methods are execrable, but when applied to children they are infinitely worse. Especially, the system of confining the children in the common jail while awaiting trial and, after conviction, of herding them with old and confirmed criminals in a punitive prison, is inevitably one of education in vice and crime. The vile infection of the place acts upon the receptive mind of the child with poisonous effect; he comes out of the prison branded with the name of criminal and yet made proud of the name. It is only in exceptional cases that such an experience fails to corrupt and pervert the child's aspirations and ideals; his whole moral nature has been deformed.

It is strange that such evils were allowed to prevail for centuries in the light of Christian civilization. The first radically effective measure for their correction in this country was an act of the legislature of the state of Illinois in the year 1899 creating a "juvenile court." The humane character and practical value of this step met with instant recognition throughout the country, and the example of Illinois was speedily followed by other states until now nearly every state in the Union has established its juvenile courts or at least a system of juvenile probation.

The Illinois Act of 1899 was entitled "An Act to regulate the treatment and control of dependent, neglected and delinquent children," and applies to male children under seventeen years of age and to female children under eighteen.

The following is a condensed summary of the act as subsequently amended: it vests jurisdiction, in all cases coming within the terms of the act, in the circuit and county courts of the state; and the judges of the circuit court, in each county having over 500,000 population, are directed to designate one or more of their number to preside over the juvenile court. Any reputable resident of the county having knowledge of a child in the county who appears to be either neglected, dependent or delinquent (as these terms are defined in the act) can file in the court a verified petition setting forth the facts. A summons is then to be issued requiring the person having custody of the child to appear with the child before the court. The parents, guardian, or some relative of the child are to be notified of the proceedings, and the attendance of the persons so summoned and notified can be enforced, if necessary, by warrant. The court then proceeds to hear and dispose of the case in a summary manner. Pending the final disposition of the case, the child may be retained in the possession of the person having charge of the same or be kept in some suitable place provided by the authorities. The court is authorized to appoint probation officers, one of whom shall be present when the child is brought before the court; shall make investigation of the facts and shall represent the interest of the child when the case is heard, furnishing such information and assistance as the judge may require; and after the trial such probation officer shall take such charge of the child as may be directed by the court.

The court, if it finds the child to be neglected, dependent or delinquent, may allow the child to remain in its own home, subject

78

to the friendly visitation of a probation officer. But if the court finds that the child's parents or custodian are unfit to care for it, and that it is for the interest of the child and the public that such child be taken from the custody of its parents or custodian (or with the parents' consent), the court may appoint some reputable citizen as its guardian and direct such guardian to place the child in some family home, or the court may commit the child to some institution or school fitted and accredited for that purpose. In the latter case some officer of the institution or school is appointed guardian to care for and educate the child. The court may in its discretion, in case of a delinquent child, permit such child to be proceeded against according to the laws governing the commission of crimes or violation of ordinances. The court may order the guardian to place the child in a hospital for treatment when the child's health requires it. Guardianship under the act shall not continue after the child reaches the age of twenty-one years, and may be sooner discharged. The separation of the child from its home is to be continued no longer than is demanded by the child's welfare. The guardian is required to make reports to the court, which has the power to remove him and appoint another in his stead, or to remove the child from one institution to another or to restore it to its parents.

Whenever a child is arrested, it is to be taken before the juvenile court, which shall dispose of the case as if the child had been brought in upon petition. No child under twelve years of age shall be committed to a jail or police station, but such child, if unable to give bail, shall be kept in some suitable place provided by the city or county outside the enclosure of any jail or police station. Any child sentenced to an institution to which adult convicts are sentenced shall not be confined in, or brought into, the same building, yard or enclosure with such adult convicts.

The act contains provisions requiring the board of public charities to inspect and supervise the institutions for the care of dependent, neglected or delinquent children, and such children are to be committed only to institutions approved and accredited by said board. The act gives power to the court to authorize the legal adoption of the child upon the consent of the parents, but the court can make the order without consent if both the parents are unfit to have the child. The court has power also to inquire into the ability of the parents of any child neglected, dependent or delinquent, to support such child and, if it finds that they are able, to enter and enforce such decree as may be equitable. The concluding section of the original act was as follows:

"This Act shall be liberally construed, to the end that its purpose may be carried out, to wit: that the care, custody and discipline of a child shall approximate, as nearly as may be, that which should be given by its parents and, in all cases where it can properly be done, the child be placed in an improved family home and become a member of the family by legal adoption or otherwise."

The act was supplemented by a further law in 1905, which enacted that the parents, guardian or custodian of any dependent, neglected or delinquent child or any other person who should knowingly do any act that directly contributed to the conditions which rendered the child dependent, neglected or delinquent, or who, having custody of the child, should, when able to do so, neglect to remove such conditions, should be deemed guilty of a misdemeanor, subject to fine and imprisonment; the court was empowered, however, to suspend sentence and release the defendant on probation for one year upon a recognizance conditioned that the defendant should provide and care for the child as directed by the court.

These laws of the state of Illinois have been set forth with some detail because in their substantial features they have been generally followed by the other states which have established juvenile courts. There have, however, been variations from the standard set by Illinois, some for the better and some for the worse.

The limitation of the age of children under jurisdiction of the juvenile court originally fixed by the Illinois statute was "under sixteen"; but this has been, by subsequent amendment, enlarged to seventeen years in the case of boys and eighteen in the case of girls, as stated above. This limit is higher than in most of the other states, except Utah where it is fixed at eighteen years for delinquent children of both sexes, and Michigan where, it would appear, any "minor" may be adjudged a dependent or neglected child. In most of the states the limit is set at sixteen years of age for both boys and girls. The limitation at twelve years as the age under which children shall not be confined in any jail or police station is much too low; the highest limit set by any state in this regard is seventeen years in Iowa and the District of Columbia. It would seem that no child under the age of twenty-one years ought to be confined in any jail or police station; and many of our jails and police stations are in such a condition that no one over the age of twenty-one, either, ought to be confined in them.

The Illinois statute applies to all children within the prescribed age (except those who are inmates of correctional institutions) irrespective of the nature of the charge that may be brought against them. In some of the states an exception is made of children who are charged with a crime punishable by death or by life imprisonment. And most of the acts creating juvenile courts empower the judge in his discretion to send any case to the criminal courts to be disposed of in the regular course of procedure.

The laws of Illinois make the juvenile courts parts of the circuit and county courts. The circuit and county courts have general and original jurisdiction in law and equity. In some of the states a new special court has been created, designated the "Juvenile Court." In a very few states, the juvenile court has been made a branch of a court having only criminal jurisdiction. The manner in which the juvenile court should be constituted and the question whether it should be regarded as a *criminal* court are matters of the most vital importance. Their solution depends upon the conception entertained regarding the proper aims and the essential functions of a children's court.

The judge of one of these courts has expressed his view of the purposes for which his court was established as follows:

"To save children from lifelong consequences of childish errors; to check their feet at the very entrance of the downward road; . . . to let them expiate a fault at their own homes under the surveillance of kindly probation officers and to accomplish these ends without the publicity that tends to blast later attempts at well-doing, as well as to save young souls from the taint of contact with matured criminals."

The practical value of such a court is more by way of prevention than of punishment. The child is taken at that plastic age when (some one has well said) "formation" and not "reformation" is the end to be aimed at. What is most carefully to be avoided is the treatment of the child as a criminal. If the children of the vicinage come to regard the juvenile court as a criminal court and brand as a criminal every child who is brought under its ministrations, its usefulness will be sadly impaired. Its true function is to appeal to the child's better nature, to develop self-respect and self-control, to exert a firm but kindly restraint, to awaken worthy motives by sympathetic encouragement. There are cases, of course, which demand rigorous treatment, but in most instances better results will follow gentler methods. Throughout the whole community the juvenile court should be looked upon as a beneficent child-saving institution, not at all as a Draconian tribunal for the punishment of children.

The wisdom, then, is apparent of making the juvenile court a branch of an established court that has civil jurisdiction, general jurisdiction in law and equity. Its powers should be of the broadest kind, and occasion may well arise for the exercise of the functions pertaining to a court of equity. Equity (as distinguished from law) takes special cognizance of domestic relations and has peculiar care over the rights of children. A court of equity holds all minor children brought within it as its special wards. Every case coming before the juvenile court involves the parents (if there are any living) as well as the child; the child cannot be treated or even considered apart from his parents and his home. Whether it is a neglected or a delinquent child, he has generally been made such through some fault or neglect of his parents; and, in order to deal properly with the child, it is imperative that the court should have power to deal with the parents. It should have power to arraign the parents and to coerce them in the performance of their duty toward their children. This often involves the surveillance of the home and its rehabilitation, to make it an abode fit for the growing child. But where the home conditions are essentially debasing, the juvenile court must have the power to take the child away from its parents and place it under influences that are healthful for both the body and the soul.

The child may be subjected to corrupting tendencies outside the home. It may be in contact with older persons who are exerting a hurtful influence and leading the child into vicious ways and habits. The juvenile court needs the power to protect the child by haling before it all persons, whoever they may be, whose association with the child is proved to be baleful, by holding such persons to a stern accountability, and by subjecting them to most drastic treatment in order that their corrupting influence over the child may be stopped. It may well be that neither the persons thus dealt with nor the parents may have been guilty of any statutory offense under the criminal law that would bring them within the jurisdiction of a criminal court; it needs a court of plenary power, with all the resources of chancery jurisdiction, that can throw its protecting arms around the child and effectually shield it from harm.

These ends were reached in the legislation of Illinois; first, by making the juvenile court a branch of an established court invested with original and general jurisdiction in law and equity; and sec-

82

CHILDREN'S COURTS AND PROBATION OFFICERS

ondly, by the supplementary act (abstracted above) which empowered the court to punish the parents or any other person who, by act or by neglect, were accountable for the conditions which rendered the child dependent, neglected or delinquent. Most of the states which have established juvenile courts have shown the wisdom of following the example of Illinois in both the particulars mentioned. Some of the states, however, as above stated, have made the juvenile court a branch of an established court having jurisdiction over criminal cases only; and some of the states have confined the jurisdiction of the juvenile court to "delinquent" children only, leaving dependent and neglected children to the mercies of private charity and public institutions.

The usefulness of the juvenile court is, of course, dependent, in the largest sense, upon the personal character of its presiding judge; it demands peculiar, and indeed exceptional, qualities,— ability to comprehend the child's point of view and to enter sympathetically into the child's motives and feelings; power to win the child's confidence and to exert the personal influence thus gained with tact and wisdom; and over all, a disposition to temper justice with extreme mercy. These are qualities that the experience gained by a judge in an ordinary criminal court is not likely to develop. On the contrary, the judge is there brought into contact with the worst side of human nature where mercy may often mean weakness; his sense of duty must often compel him to stifle his sympathies, and the general attitude of mind in which a conscientious judge comes to regard the prisoners brought before him in the criminal court is profoundly different from the paternal spirit that ought to govern the judge who deals with children.

The exclusion of dependent and neglected children from the juvenile court, and the confinement of its jurisdiction to delinquent children only, as well as the establishment of that court as a part of a criminal court, appear to be unfortunate and mistaken variants from the Illinois precedent. Neglect is the germ of delinquency, and to remedy or cure neglect is the best preventive of delinquency. Private charity tries to cure neglect and to improve the home, but charity can issue no mandates that must be obeyed. In the last resort and when the case becomes extreme, public authority puts the neglected child into the poor-house or a public institution. The juvenile court is brought into immediate contact with the neglected home and can exert there its uplifting and renovating power with an authority that no other agency can command. All the juvenile court laws recognize the fact that the home is the natural place where the child ought to grow up. These laws contemplate every effort to improve the defective home so that it shall be made a fit abode for the child; and it is only when all efforts have failed that the juvenile court as a foster parent takes the child away from its home and its parents and creates for him a more wholesome environment. This is one of the most valuable functions of a juvenile court, and it seems a pity that some states have restricted its jurisdiction to delinquent children.

But even the states which have made the juvenile court a criminal court and have confined its action to cases of delinquency, have been careful to segregate it from the other courts. In some states, the laws require a separate building, remote from the criminal courts, for the exclusive occupancy of the juvenile court; in others, the law directs that a separate room shall be set apart for the sessions of the juvenile court and has provisions for securing its privacy, for guarding from public knowledge the names of the children brought before it and from giving publicity to its proceedings in special cases. These provisions are prompted by a tender solicitude to save the children from the taint of any public disgrace. Nearly all the acts contain a rigid prohibition of the confinement of a child in any jail or police station; this, with other provisions in the acts, involves the necessity of providing buildings in which the children can (in case of necessity) be confined while awaiting trial, and industrial and training schools to which they may be committed when taken away from their homes.

The example of Illinois is followed in most of the states by allowing any reputable citizen to bring a case before the juvenile court; but a few of the states have restricted this right to the district attorney or a probation officer. By this restriction, every complaint receives some preliminary examination by a responsible official and the court is thus relieved from petitions that are baseless or frivolous or animated by malice only.

The juvenile court laws bear close relation to the child labor laws and the school laws regarding truancy. The child labor laws aim to protect children from excessive toil unfitted to their years. But it must not be forgotten that a child, as well as an adult, needs employment. It needs recreation and play, fatigue and rest, but sheer aimless idleness is fraught with danger. Systematic exercise of body and mind is the condition of healthy development; and vacuous idleness leads to moral degeneracy as surely as overwork results in

84

physical degeneracy. The compulsory school laws thus supplement the child labor laws.

In the city of Denver, the juvenile court is in constant communication with the public schools. Whenever a scholar comes before the juvenile court and is placed under probation, the authorities of the school which he attends are notified of the fact; and if on any day he fails to appear at school, his absence is reported to the court and the probation officer having the case in charge promptly sets out in pursuit of the truant. The teachers also keep the court informed of the school record of the probationers, giving details of their conduct and progress or failures. Occasional meetings are held where the judge meets the principals and teachers of the school with the probation officers, and they confer together regarding the needs of the scholars under probation and the special treatment best adapted to each case. In this way, the schools become a powerful auxiliary of the juvenile court. Similar relations might most advantageously be established between the court and the proprietors of factories or offices where children under probation are employed at work. Judge Lindsey of the Denver juvenile court is a man of very exceptional personal qualities which enable him so to win the hearts of the boys brought before him, that there is excited within them a sense of duty and loyalty; the boys themselves are thus transformed into co-workers with the court and in very many instances have been led to exert a most beneficent influence over their associates.

The juvenile court needs another auxiliary which is not provided by the laws of any of the states. The nearest approach to supplying this need is a provision contained in most of the juvenile court laws empowering the court to place a child brought before it in a hospital when the child's health or condition requires it. But there are many children, not needing hospital treatment, who do urgently need medical attention and care. Numerous cases of juvenile delinquency are traced to bodily defects or vicious practices which occasion ill temper, irritability and lack of control. Imperfect vision, decayed teeth, deranged nerves, disordered digestion, adenoids, malformations, with a thousand other ills to which flesh is heir, if treated in childhood, are often entirely remedied by medical skill; and thus, in very many instances, a vicious, stupid boy or girl is transformed into a bright, cheerful, exemplary child. Wonders have been achieved in this direction, even with adult subjects, in the Elmira Reformatory, by medical treatment, with baths, massage, diet, athletic exercise. The experiments made there afford a striking demonstration of the possibility of brightening dull intellects and awakening dormant sensibilities by physical agencies. Every juvenile court ought to have a medical department; it is needed, not less than it is by a life insurance company, to furnish a basis of judgment and of prognosis in each individual case. Every child brought into the court should undergo a searching physical examination by a competent physician who should be an officer of the court; his report and his counsel would be an invaluable aid to the court in comprehending the case and in making intelligent disposition of it.

The most valuable and powerful instrument at the service of the juvenile court is one to which only incidental reference has thus far been made; this is the probation system. The consideration of it has been reserved to the last because the system applies to adults as well as to children and it is necessary to treat it in its two-fold application.

When a person is brought to trial and proved to be guilty of the offense charged, the court may proceed to pronounce sentence or, in the discretion of the judge, may suspend or defer the sentence and release the defendant on such conditions as may be imposed. This latter course is pursued, naturally, only in cases where there are mitigating circumstances and the judge has reason to believe that the defendant will not again commit an offense against the law and may safely be given another chance without further punishment. Such release under suspension of sentence has long been within the power of the criminal court and the practice has widely prevailed. Before the adoption of the statutes relating to "probation," the release on suspended sentence amounted practically in most cases to an unconditional discharge; because, whatever might be the conditions imposed, the court was without any adequate agency to follow the subsequent career of the defendant and to see that the conditions were performed. Often, it was only when the defendant committed another offense and chanced to be brought again before the same judge and his identity with the previous defendant happened to be recognized, that it became known that he had violated the conditions under which the clemency of the court had been extended to him; the suspended sentence was then revived and the defendant was sentenced and committed for the first offense. This situation made it difficult to know whether the suspension of sentence in any given case had proved to be advantageous or injurious; it was impossible to gain reliable data on which to determine under what circumstances suspension of the sentence would be judicious and even whether the practice of suspending sentence at all was advisable. The need was pressing for an additional officer of the court, armed with authority from the court, to exercise supervision over offenders released on probation and to encourage them by friendly aid and counsel in their effort to lead an upright life.

The state of Massachusetts took the lead in this direction by passing an act in 1869, which required the governor to appoint a "visiting agent" whose duties were prescribed by the act. Whenever application was made for the commitment of any child, one week's previous notice of the hearing was to be given by the magistrate to the visiting agent who was required to attend at the hearing; if it then appeared to the magistrate that the interests of the child would be promoted by placing him in a suitable family instead of sending him to a reformatory, the magistrate might authorize the board of state charities to indenture the child or to place him in such family. It was made the duty of the agent to seek out families suitable for receiving such children and, generally, to visit the children and make monthly reports to the board of state charities. This act was confined to juvenile probation; but in 1878, Massachusetts enacted a law for placing on probation, under the care of probation officers, such adults charged with or convicted of crime as might "reasonably be expected to be reformed without punishment." This latter act was a local one applying only to the county which includes the city of Boston; but it was followed in 1880 by an act extending the probation system to all the other cities and towns of the state. The very successful results attending the operation of the system in Massachusetts excited interest throughout the country, and the example set by that state has led to the establishment of a system of probation with probation officers in more than three-quarters of the states of the Union.

The duties of a probation officer are substantially the same in all the states which have adopted the system. The first duty is one of investigation; whenever a person, adult or juvenile, is brought before the court, the probation officer must ascertain, from sources outside the person himself, all that he can learn regarding the occupation, habits, family, associations, the whole environment of the person in question. The information thus gained is indispensable in enabling the magistrate to make an intelligent disposition of the case; it is necessary through all the proceedings, both before and after the hearing, that the probation officer and the magistrate should counsel together and keep in close touch with each other as well as with the probationer. When the hearing has been had, and the person accused and found guilty is released on probation, it is the duty of the probation officer to render such assistance as he can in securing employment for the probationer and to see to it that the conditions of his release are faithfully performed; he should try to get into sympathetic touch with the probationer and to influence him by kindly encouragement and aid to avoid evil associations and to lead a better life. The probation officer must report to the court from time to time upon the probationer's progress; and the probationer receives an absolute release when he has performed the conditions imposed by the court and has demonstrated his ability and his purpose to live within the law. But if the probationer proves irresponsive to the clemency of the court and persists in evil ways, the probation officer is empowered to arrest him and to bring him before the court where the sentence of condemnation, which had been suspended, will be pronounced and its execution enforced.

In administering the probation system, it is essential (especially in the case of adults) that the probationer should realize that he is under the power and the condemnation of the court and that the law cannot be violated with impunity; he should realize that the probation officer, though in the truest sense his friend, is invested with an authority which the probationer must obey and cannot resist. He should understand that probation does not mean judicial weakness, that it does not place him in the realm of mere moral suasion which he can defy, but that it holds him in a position where his passions and habits and tendencies which are evil *must* be subdued. The correction of his life is all that can save him from imprisonment and lasting disgrace. Thus the motive of deterrence is presented in its most imperative form.

Release on *probation* and release on *parole* have substantially the same meaning. Both imply a certain clemency by which an offender is released before he has the right by the letter of the law to demand his release; and in both cases the release is granted to test the offender and with the belief that he will abstain from crime. By accepted usage, however, the two words have distinctly separate meanings. *Probation* is applied only to persons released before imprisonment and then committed to the care of a probation officer. This may occur before sentence, the sentence being suspended, or after sentence, the execution of the sentence being suspended; but, in every case, before the offender is committed to prison. *Parole,*

88

on the other hand, is applied to persons committed to prison under an indeterminate sentence, or its equivalent, and released at some point between the minimum and maximum limits of the sentence. The use of probation officers to supervise and care for adult prisoners on parole has not secured general adoption. A discharged convict, however, coming out of prison after a long seclusion from the world, surely needs the kindly services and counsel of a friend to aid him in beginning life anew; and the need is quite as imperative as in the case of those offenders who are not burdened with the disabilities and the stigma that handicap an ex-convict. It is to be hoped that the probation system may be universally extended so that convicts discharged from prison upon parole may not be exposed unaided and alone to the reluctant mercies of the world, but may be committed to the care and supervision of a probation officer; that would give the ex-convict in his helplessness one responsible friend on whom he could lean for sympathetic encouragement and aid.

In the probation laws of some of the states, provision is made to enable probation officers to expend, when necessary, small sums of money for the relief of their probationers. While the expenditure of money in relief work should be sparing and limited, cases must often arise when the probation officer cannot possibly perform toward his ward the common duties of humanity without making some pecuniary outlay. Whatever restraint the law may put upon the probation officer in this regard, it is absolutely essential to the successful discharge of his duties that he should be provided with funds the disbursement of which must be left measurably to his discretion. Every probation officer should possess a character of such unimpeachable integrity that his account of "expenses" may be audited in a liberal spirit.

What other qualities are needed to make a successful probation officer? He must have force of character and a dignity in keeping with his official authority in order that he may command the respect of his ward. He must have a mind well balanced and a high moral sense, that he may prove a judicious counsellor. He must possess genial qualities and a sympathetic nature, that he may gain the confidence of his ward and be able to influence his conduct. It may well be asked how, with all these requirements, any person can be found willing to undertake, as a volunteer without remuneration, the arduous responsibilities of the probation officer. It is only because such a volunteer is animated by another essential qualification, a devoted spirit of altruism, the highest development of which has been called the "enthusiasm for humanity." But the possession of this enthusiasm alone is far from being a sufficient qualification. There is many a person of most worthy and devoted, but wholly tactless, character whose ministrations as a probation officer, though governed by the very kindest intentions, would drive his probationer certainly to drink and possibly to murder. Perhaps the supreme condition of success for a probation officer is the possession of *tact;* for tactfulness really comprises most of the other qualifications—a sound judgment, a kind and genial temper, a knowledge of human nature, and skill in influencing men. It is obvious that the value of a probation system depends very largely upon the personal fitness of those who are appointed probation officers.

It becomes a question, then, vital to the whole system, In whom shall the law vest the power of appointing probation officers and what rules or tests shall be applied to govern their selection?

In some states, the laws provide that members of the police force may be selected and detailed to perform the work of probation officers in the several courts. This provision can hardly be dictated by any motive but that of economy; it saves the payment of salaries to probation officers. Policemen, in the eyes of the humbler classes and especially in the eyes of those who have lawless tendencies, are the ministers of judgment and not of mercy; they are avoided with fear and suspicion. An offender against the law would certainly be reluctant to accept a policeman as a "big brother." The office of policeman is essentially inconsistent with that of probation officer. The duties of the police lie in the detection of crime and the rigid enforcement of law; all their training and experience unfit them for the confidential and sympathetic relation of probation officer and ward.

The relative merits of volunteer and salaried probation officers have been debated with a resulting conflict of opinion. Where a person is willing to devote himself to rendering friendly service and aid to one in need, without hope of reward, it furnishes convincing evidence of such disinterested kindness as can hardly fail to be met with appreciation and grateful response by the recipient. The same service and aid coming from a salaried officer might be received with indifference as a mere official act which the officer was paid to perform. On the other hand, a volunteer, subject to the superior demands made upon him by his business and private affairs, may find it impossible to devote the time required, especially in cases of emergency, to meet the needs of his ward. The volunteer, moreover, must necessarily lack the wide and varied experience which is gained by the officer who devotes his entire time and energies to the service and thus becomes a skilled expert. On the whole, the weight of authority appears to favor the employment of salaried officers, as necessary to secure the systematic organization and efficient conduct of the probation work. At the same time, the services of volunteers are not to be indiscriminately rejected; there are many special cases in which a competent volunteer may be able to effect results beyond the power of a paid officer.

The office of probation officer comes within the civil service laws of some of the states, which determine the eligibility of candidates by competitive examination. The examination consists of written answers to printed questions. A candidate may be able to describe glibly all the duties of the office and the qualifications needed to make a good officer, and yet may not himself possess the personal qualities essential to competency. It is difficult to believe that any written examination can be devised which will afford a reliable method of selection. It is a question of personal qualities and of individual character and experience, far more than of mental attainments. If the examination should be conducted with the aid of persons experienced in probation work and supplemented by oral examination, it is possible that satisfactory results might be obtained under the civil service rules. But a better mode of selection seems to be through the action of a local probation board, as the subject will be treated later.

In most of the states, the power of appointing probation officers for the court in which they are to serve is given to the judge or judges of that court. There is the danger attaching to all judicial appointments, that they may be treated as a matter of patronage and political preferment. This danger is more imminent in the criminal than in the civil courts, because the selection of criminal judges is generally apt to be governed by personal influence and political expediency to a greater extent than is the selection of candidates for the higher civil courts. It cannot be denied that, while there are many criminal judges of the very highest character and ability, there are some judges presiding over the lower criminal courts who are wholly unfit to be trusted with the appointment of probation officers. But it is an objection, perhaps even more serious, to this mode of selection by judicial appointment, especially in large cities having numerous courts with varying jurisdiction and practice, that each court becomes a law unto itself; the probation officers of each court, governed by the special rules of that court, are brought into no relation with like officers of other courts. The result is segregated effort; lack of system, lack of developed progress, lack of inspiration, needs that can be supplied only by centralized organization.

The probation work that is scattered over a large city should be co-ordinated and unified by being brought under the supervision of a central city board of probation. The members of such board should be versed in the principles of penology, and possess a comprehensive knowledge of the approved methods in conducting charitable and philanthropic enterprises; more than that, they should have had practical experience, through personal engagement in benevolent work, to give them a sympathetic understanding of the objects and the needs of the probation system. To this municipal board of experts could safely be intrusted the selection and appointment of probation officers for the city. Under the supervision of this board, the probation officers should hold periodical meetings, where they would be brought into contact with each other, profit by each other's experiences, discuss methods, and gain new inspiration and devotion for their work. By the central board there could be introduced into the system throughout the city methods of co-operation and co-ordination which would add to the efficiency of its administration; means of identification could be secured, which would prevent the repeated release by different courts of the same probationer; and the whole operation of the probation system, by being effectively systematized, would be made progressive.

In 1905, the legislature of New York created a commission to examine and report on the subject of probation. The following year, the commission, of which Mr. Homer Folks was chairman, made a most admirable and exhaustive report. To this report the present writer is indebted for the suggestion, just made, of a municipal probation board and also for a flood of light on many of the topics discussed in this chapter. The commission prepared and recommended for adoption a very carefully digested series of statutes covering the whole system of probation. The proposed municipal board for the city of New York was to consist of seven members appointed by the mayor, and it was recommended that they be selected from a list of fourteen candidates to be nominated by five designated charitable organizations. The commission also recommended the creation of a permanent state department of probation, which should investigate the proceedings of all municipal boards and of probation officers and inquire into their conduct and efficiency, make rules and regulations regarding probation methods, collect statistical information as to the system and, in an annual report to the legislature, make suggestions or recommendations looking to the improvement and development of the probation system. It is cause for regret that the legislature of New York has thus far failed to adopt the comprehensive acts proposed by the commission; but in 1907, the legislature did enact a law creating a permanent state probation commission which was vested with substantially the same powers and duties that had been recommended in that behalf by the first mentioned commission. The state probation commission thus created consists of seven members, four of whom are appointed by the governor, two are designated, one by the state board of charities, and one by the state commission of prisons, and the remaining member is the commissioner of education *ex officio*. Very fortunately Mr. Folks is the president of this New York State Probation Commission, which is now doing most thorough and fruitful work. Permanent state boards of probation, with similar powers, have been created in several other states of the Union.

The probation system, in most of the states where it is established, has been introduced within the last decade, and is therefore a comparatively new feature in their jurisprudence. But it has stood the test of trial and, by constantly extending experience, its methods are being more fully developed and improved and its practical value is being more and more conclusively demonstrated. There is reasonable ground for hope that the wider adoption and progressive growth (which are confidently anticipated) of the two correlated institutions of probation and the juvenile court, may produce, in the not distant future, very striking results in the repression and reduction of crime in the United States.

CHAPTER VII

CRIMINAL PROCEDURE IN THE UNITED STATES

THE methods and forms of legal procedure in criminal prosecutions vary in the different states and, for that matter, even in different courts of the same state. But these variances are, for the most part, so far superficial and formal, that substantial uniformity in criminal procedure may be said to prevail throughout the Union. As illustrative of what may thus be termed American procedure, it may be useful to trace in detail the course of a criminal prosecution through its successive stages from its inception to the execution of final judgment. For this purpose, the system established in the state of New York has been selected, not merely because of the relative importance and prestige which that state has attained in the general field of jurisprudence, but because its legal codes have been widely adopted or followed in many of its sister states. For these reasons, it is thought that the system practised in New York will be found to be more nearly typical than any other, of the prevailing criminal procedure in the United States.

For minor offenses, the procedure is simple and summary; such cases are brought directly to trial and final judgment before inferior courts of criminal jurisdiction. They may, however, in some instances be removed from the inferior court and be prosecuted by indictment in a higher court upon the certificate of a judge of the higher court that such course is reasonable. When the trial is had in the inferior court, resulting in conviction, the defendant has the right of appeal only when allowed by a judge of a superior court.

For felonies and grave misdemeanors, the procedure is more complex and tortuous. The following condensed summary aims to set forth in outline the principal successive steps of a prosecution "by information and indictment."

THE INFORMATION

When an information is laid before a magistrate that a person has been guilty of some designated crime, the magistrate must examine on oath the informant and any witnesses he may produce,

94

taking their depositions in writing. If the magistrate is satisfied that a crime has been committed, and that there is reasonable cause to believe that the person accused has committed it, he must issue a warrant for the arrest of the person, directing that he (the defendant) be brought before him, or, if the offense was a misdemeanor committed in another town, before a magistrate of such town. The warrant, if issued by a magistrate of inferior criminal jurisdiction, can be executed within the county in which it is issued; if the defendant is in another county, the warrant can be executed there only upon the written direction of a magistrate of that county indorsed on the warrant. If issued by the judge of a court not of inferior jurisdiction, the warrant can be executed without further indorsement anywhere within the state.

THE ARREST

The officer receiving the warrant must arrest the defendant; the arrest can be made on any day and at any time of day or night, in case of a felony, but, in case of a misdemeanor, the arrest cannot be made on Sunday or at night, unless by special direction of the magistrate. The officer making the arrest must inform the defendant of the warrant and must show it to him, if required.

An arrest may also be made by an officer, or by a private person, without a warrant, for a crime committed or attempted in his presence, or when the person arrested has committed a felony, although not committed in the presence of the one making the arrest.

THE EXAMINATION

When the defendant is brought before the magistrate, the magistrate must inform him of the charge against him and of his right to the aid of legal counsel before any further proceedings, and must allow the defendant a reasonable time, and provide a messenger, to send for counsel. Upon the appearance of counsel or after waiting a reasonable time therefor, the magistrate must proceed to examine the case. He must first read to the defendant the depositions taken upon the original information, and must upon request summon the deponents (if within the county) for cross-examination, and must issue subpoenas for the attendance of any additional witnesses required by the prosecutor or the defendant. The defendant must be informed that he has the right to make a statement (to be reduced to writing) answering the charge and explaining the facts alleged against him, but that his failure to make such statement cannot be used against him on the trial. The testimony of all the witnesses

95

must be reduced to writing, be signed by the witnesses and be authenticated and certified by the magistrate. The depositions must be kept from the public, but the defendant is entitled to a copy of them.

DEFENDANT DISCHARGED OR "HELD TO ANSWER"

After hearing the proofs, if it appear to the magistrate either that a crime has not been committed or that there is not sufficient cause to believe the defendant guilty, the magistrate must discharge the defendant. On the other hand, if it appear from the examination that a crime has been committed, and that there is sufficient cause to believe the defendant guilty thereof, the magistrate must indorse on the depositions an order that the defendant be "held to answer the same," and must commit the defendant to custody, unless bail is given in case the offense is a bailable one.

BAIL

The provisions relating to bail, at this stage, apply at all the subsequent stages of a criminal process down to the final conviction, and may be here stated once for all. The admission of the defendant to bail before conviction is a matter of right in cases of misdemeanor; in all other cases it is a matter resting in the discretion of the court. If the crime is one punishable with death, or such that, if death should ensue, the crime would be murder, bail can be allowed only by a justice of the Supreme Court. In lieu of a bondsman, the defendant may make a deposit of money with the county treasurer in the amount named in the order admitting him to bail. After conviction of a crime not punishable with death, and an appeal therefrom with stay of proceedings, the defendant may still be admitted to bail as a matter of right, if the appeal be from a judgment imposing a fine, and as a matter of discretion in all other cases. If the defendant fails to give bail or to deposit money in lieu thereof in any instance where it is allowed, he is, of course, committed and kept in custody.

DISPOSITION OF CASE FOR TRIAL

In certain cases where the offense is a minor misdemeanor the defendant can elect to be tried at once by a court of inferior jurisdiction. If he does not so elect, then in every case the magistrate must, within five days after the conclusion of the examination, transmit to the clerk of a court having power to inquire into offenses by the intervention of a grand jury, the warrant of arrest, all the depositions, the statement of the defendant if any, and all undertakings given.

GRAND JURY

The case next comes before a grand jury, which proceeds to investigate the charge in secret session. A grand jury is appurtenant to, and subject to the direction of, a court of not inferior jurisdiction; and the code contains elaborate provisions governing the drawing, the summoning and the sessions of a grand jury, and regulating the conduct of its proceedings. The grand jury consists of not more than twenty-three, nor less than sixteen, members, of whom twelve only are required to concur in finding an indictment.

The depositions (and statement of the defendant) taken before the magistrate by whom the defendant was held to answer are submitted to the grand jury, who receive also the testimony of witnesses produced before them, as well as legal documentary evidence. The grand jury is not bound to hear evidence for the defendant; but it is their duty to weigh all the evidence submitted to them, and when they have reason to believe that other evidence within their reach will explain away the charge, they should order such evidence to be produced; and, for that purpose, may require the district attorney to issue process for the witnesses. When all the evidence before them is such as in their judgment would, if unexplained or uncontradicted, warrant a conviction of the defendant, it is the duty of the grand jury to find an indictment, which is defined as an accusation in writing, presented to the court, charging the defendant with a specified crime. The indictment must contain the title of the action, specifying the name of the court to which the indictment is presented, the names of the parties, and a plain and concise statement of the act constituting the crime, which crime must be one which was committed, or which is triable, within the jurisdiction of the court. And there must be indorsed upon it the names of the witnesses examined before the grand jury, and of those whose depositions have been read before them. The indictment, when completed, must be filed with the clerk of the court and must not be shown to any person (other than a public officer) until the defendant has been arrested or has appeared. If twelve grand jurors do not concur in finding an indictment, the depositions and statement transmitted to them must be returned to the court, with an indorsement that the charge is dismissed. The charge cannot then be again submitted to a grand jury, unless the court shall specially so direct.

ARRAIGNMENT OF THE DEFENDANT

When the indictment is filed, the defendant is brought before the court to answer; if the crime charged be a felony, he must appear in person; if it be a misdemeanor, he may appear by counsel. If the defendant appear without counsel, the court must, if desired by the defendant, assign counsel to act in his behalf. If the defendant fail to appear, or is absent when his personal attendance is necessary, the clerk of the court (acting upon the direction of the court or upon the application of the district attorney), or the district attorney himself, may issue a bench warrant for the arrest of the defendant.

The arraignment consists in stating to the defendant the charge in the indictment and asking him whether he pleads guilty or not guilty thereto. The defendant, for answer, may so plead, or he may move the court to set aside the indictment or may demur thereto.

The motion to set aside the indictment must be based upon alleged irregularities in the proceedings before the grand jury. If the motion is granted, the court may discharge the defendant, or direct that the case be resubmitted to the same or another grand jury, the defendant meantime remaining in custody. An order setting aside an indictment is no bar to a future prosecution for the same offense. If the motion is denied, the defendant must immediately plead or demur to the indictment.

ANSWER TO INDICTMENT

The defendant may demur to the indictment when it appears, upon its face, that the defendant ought not to be convicted, by reason of jurisdictional defects, or because the facts stated are legally insufficient to show that he has committed a crime. If the demurrer is allowed, the judgment is final and is a bar to another prosecution for the same offense, unless the court deems the objection on which the demurrer is based to be avoidable in a new indictment, and directs the case to be resubmitted to the same or another grand jury. If the demurrer is disallowed, the court permits the defendant to plead to the indictment. If he fails to plead, judgment is pronounced against him if the crime charged is a misdemeanor, otherwise a plea of "not guilty" must be entered.

The plea to an indictment may be "guilty" (of the crime charged or of any lesser crime) or "not guilty," or a plea of a former conviction or acquittal of the crime charged. But if the crime charged is one that may be punishable by death, a conviction cannot be had upon a plea of guilty. The plea of guilty can be put in only by the defendant in person, and not by his counsel, except where the indictment is against a corporation. The plea of insanity may be presented as a specification under the plea of not guilty. If a defendant refuse to answer by either demurrer or plea, a plea of not guilty must be entered.

THE JURY

If an issue of fact has been raised, by a plea of not guilty or of a former conviction or acquittal of the same crime, the trial must be had by a jury. In securing a jury, objection may be made by the defendant to the entire list of those summoned to attend as jurors, on the ground of official irregularities in drawing or summoning them. If this objection is disallowed, individual jurors may be challenged. Objection may be made to a juror, without assigning any reason therefor; such "peremptory challenges" are allowed, where the crime is punishable with death, to the number of thirty; if punishable with imprisonment for life or for a term of ten or more years, to the number of twenty, and in all other cases to the number of five. Beside these peremptory challenges, challenges may be made without limit, on the ground that the juror has been convicted of felony, or is otherwise disqualified by law from serving as a juror, or upon the ground that the juror, from bias, prejudice or other special cause, cannot try the issue impartially. These "challenges for cause" are tried and determined by the court upon examination of the juror challenged and of other witnesses who may be called, and the first twelve persons who are approved or accepted are sworn and constitute the jury to try the issue. The law also provides for a "special jury" in peculiar cases.

THE TRIAL

If the indictment be for a felony, the defendant must be personally present at the trial; but if for a misdemeanor, the trial may be had in his absence, if he appear by counsel.

The trial is conducted in the following order of procedure:

The district attorney or counsel for the people opens the case, and offers the evidence in support of the indictment.

The defendant or his counsel opens the defense, and offers the evidence in support thereof.

The parties may then, respectively, offer rebutting testimony, but the court may in its discretion permit them to introduce additional evidence upon their original case.

When the evidence is concluded, the case may be submitted to the jury without argument, or, if the parties or either of them elect to present argument, the defendant or his counsel must begin, and the counsel for the people shall have the right to conclude the argument before the jury.

The court must then charge the jury.

The rules governing the admission of evidence in civil cases apply for the most part in criminal cases. The defendant may testify in his own behalf, but his neglect or refusal to do so shall create no presumption against him. A confession of the defendant is not sufficient to warrant his conviction without additional proof that the crime charged has been committed; nor can a conviction be had upon the uncorroborated testimony of an accomplice. If, at any time after the evidence on either side is closed, the court deem it insufficient to warrant a conviction, it may advise the jury to acquit the defendant, and they must follow the advice. The jurors may, at any time before the final submission of the cause, in the discretion of the court, be permitted to separate, or be kept in charge of proper officers, who shall be sworn to suffer no person to speak to or communicate with the jurors, nor to do so themselves, on any subject connected with the trial; and the jurors at each adjournment of the court must be admonished by the court not to converse among themselves on any subject connected with the trial, or to form or express any opinion thereon until the cause is finally submitted to them. Questions of law arising in the course of the trial must be decided by the court, and questions of fact by the jury, except that on the trial of an indictment for libel the jury have the right to determine the law and the fact.

At the close of the case, the jury, upon retiring for deliberation, may take with them notes of the testimony made by themselves, but none made by any other person; also (upon the consent of the court, the defendant and the counsel for the people), any paper or article that has been received in evidence. If the jury are unable to agree upon a verdict, the court may discharge them, and the case must be retried at the same or another term.

The defendant may take exceptions to decisions of the court upon matters of law by which his rights are prejudiced, in allowing or disallowing challenges to the jury, in admitting or rejecting witnesses or testimony, or in charging or instructing the jury, and may base an appeal upon such exceptions. (No corresponding right of exception or appeal is allowed to the counsel for the people.)

THE VERDICT

If the jury agree, their verdict may be either a general or a special one. A general verdict is one of "guilty" or "not guilty" or "for the people" or "for the defendant." A special verdict (which cannot be rendered, however, in case of libel) is one by which the jury find the facts only, setting them forth in detail in writing, and leaving the judgment to the court. If the crime is one consisting of different degrees, the jury may find the defendant not guilty of the degree charged in the indictment, but guilty of an inferior degree, or of an attempt to commit the crime. Upon a trial for murder or manslaughter, if the act complained of is not proved to be the cause of death, the defendant may be convicted of assault. A conviction on a charge of assault does not bar a subsequent prosecution for murder or manslaughter, if the person assaulted die after the conviction, in case death results from the injury caused by the assault. In all other cases, the defendant may be found guilty of any crime, the commission of which is necessarily included in the one charged in the indictment. Where there is a verdict of conviction which seems to the court to be based upon a misapprehension of the law by the jury, the court may instruct the jury further upon the law and direct them to reconsider their verdict; if, after reconsideration, the jury return the same verdict, it must be entered. But when the verdict is one of acquittal, the court cannot require the jury to reconsider it. If the defense is insanity of the defendant, the jury must be instructed, if they acquit him on that ground, to state the fact with their verdict; in such case, the court must, if it deem the defendant's discharge dangerous to the public peace or safety, order him to be committed to the state lunatic asylum until he becomes sane.

INSANITY OF DEFENDANT

When a defendant pleads insanity, the court, instead of proceeding with the trial, may appoint a commission to examine him and report as to his sanity at the time when he committed the crime. If a defendant, while in confinement under indictment, at any time before or after conviction, appear to be insane, the court may appoint a similar commission to report as to his sanity at the time of their examination. The commission must examine the defendant, and may call and examine witnesses; they must be attended by the district attorney, and the counsel for the defendant may take part in the proceedings. If the commission find the defendant insane, the trial or judgment must be suspended until he becomes sane; and the court, if it deem his discharge dangerous to the public, must order that he be, meantime, committed by the sheriff to a lunatic asylum, there to be detained until he becomes sane. When he becomes sane, the superintendent of the asylum must give notice of the fact to a judge of the court, who must require the sheriff to bring the defendant from the asylum and keep him in custody until he is brought to trial, judgment or execution, as the case may be, or until he is legally discharged.

PROCEEDINGS AFTER VERDICT AND BEFORE JUDGMENT

The defendant may move for a new trial on the ground of defects or errors in the proceedings during the trial, on the ground that the verdict is contrary to law or against the evidence, or on the ground of newly discovered evidence. If based on the ground last mentioned, the motion may be made at any time within one year, or, in case of sentence of death, at any time before execution. If a new trial is granted, all the testimony must be produced anew, and the former verdict cannot be used or referred to, either in evidence or in argument.

The defendant may also make an application that no judgment be entered, by reason of lack of jurisdiction in the court, or that the facts stated do not constitute a crime. If the application is granted, and it appears that there is not evidence sufficient to convict the defendant of any crime, he must be discharged and acquitted of the charge in the indictment. But if there is reasonable ground to believe the defendant might be found guilty upon a new indictment properly framed, he may be recommitted to answer such new indictment; and if there is reasonable ground to believe him guilty of another crime he must be held to answer therefor.

THE JUDGMENT

When judgment is rendered, the defendant must be present, if the conviction be for a felony, but if for a misdemeanor, judgment may be pronounced in his absence.

When the defendant is arraigned for judgment, he must be asked by the clerk whether he has any legal cause to show why judgment should not be pronounced against him. He may show cause and make motion either for arrest of judgment or for a new trial, whereupon the court shall proceed to decide upon such motion; or the defendant may aver that he is insane, and if the court thinks there is reasonable ground for believing him to be insane, the question of his insanity must be tried by a commission (as herein above set forth). If the defendant be found to be sane, judgment must be pronounced; but if found insane, he must be committed to the state lunatic asylum until he becomes sane; and when notice is given of that fact, he must be brought before the court for judgment.

If no sufficient cause appear to the court why judgment should not be pronounced, it must thereupon be rendered.

PROBATION

After a plea or verdict of guilty in a case where the court has a discretion as to the extent of the punishment, if it appears to the court that there are mitigating circumstances, the court has the power to place the defendant in charge of a probation officer. In such case, the court may suspend sentence, upon such terms and conditions as it shall impose, from time to time, or, if judgment is rendered requiring defendant to pay a fine or to be imprisoned until it is paid, the court upon imposing sentence may suspend its execution for such time and upon such terms as it shall determine, provided that, upon payment of the fine, the judgment shall be satisfied and the probation cease. The probation may in every case be revoked and terminated by the court at any time, and the sentence which had been suspended may be pronounced at any time before the expiration of the longest period for which the defendant might have been sentenced, and the execution of the judgment may be enforced for its unexpired term.

APPEALS

An appeal to the appellate division of the Supreme Court may be taken by the people only from a judgment sustaining defendant's demurrer to the indictment and from an order arresting a judgment of conviction. An appeal can be taken by the defendant from a judgment of conviction; such appeal must be taken to the said appellate division, except that, when the judgment is of death, the appeal is made directly to the Court of Appeals and, upon the appeal, every decision of the court in any intermediate order or proceeding may be reviewed. A further appeal may be taken from the appellate division to the Court of Appeals from a judgment affirming or reversing (1) a judgment of conviction or (2) a judgment sustaining a demurrer to an indictment or (3) an order arresting judgment, and from a final determination affecting a substantial right of defendant. These appeals

103

are matters of right, and .must be taken within one year after the judgment or order appealed from.

An appeal by the people does not stay or affect the operation of a judgment in defendant's favor until the judgment is reversed. An appeal by defendant to the appellate division stays the execution of the judgment or determination appealed from only upon a certificate signed by the judge who presided at the trial or by a justice of the Supreme Court that in his opinion there is reasonable doubt whether the judgment should stand. The appellate court in any case and the Court of Appeals when the judgment is of death, may order a new trial, if it is satisfied that the verdict against the defendant was against the weight of evidence or against law, or that justice requires a new trial, whether exceptions have been taken or not. The defendant's appeal to the Court of Appeals stays execution only upon a like certificate by a judge of that court or of the appellate division, except that, when the judgment is of death, the appeal alone effects a stay.

The court must give judgment upon the appeal without regard to technical errors or defects or to exceptions not affecting substantial rights. The court may correct an erroneous judgment to conform to the verdict or finding, and, in case of reversal, may order a new trial which must proceed in all respects as if no trial had been had.

The course thus briefly traced, certainly presents a long and devious path for a prosecuting officer to tread without making a single misstep. At the trial, especially, the examination of witnesses, when opposed by an alert advocate on the part of the defendant, gives rise to endless rulings and exceptions relating to the admission of testimony. It is a severe test of the skill of a prosecuting attorney and of the astuteness of a presiding judge to conduct a criminal prosecution to its end without committing any reversible error.

The procedure, in its main features, is based upon the Common Law, which is generally regarded as invested with a certain degree of sanctity. But it must be remembered that the Common Law system of criminal procedure was developed in turbulent times, when the people of England were struggling to protect their liberty against encroachments by the crown, when courts and judges, who held their office by royal appointment, were corrupt; when the machinery of the criminal law was often used oppressively to compass political ends and to further despotic measures; in times, too, when crime was widely prevalent throughout the country and the punishments of crime were excessively severe and merciless, all felonies being punishable by death. It followed inevitably that the current of popular sympathy ran strongly for the prisoner at the bar. And it is not at all surprising that the forms of criminal procedure came to be so moulded by the Common Law as to throw every safeguard around the person accused of crime. Not only was he presumed to be innocent, but throughout the prosecution he was awarded certain positive advantages over the prosecutor, which were designed to preclude the possibility of a conviction, if the prisoner were indeed innocent in fact.

The danger of oppression by the sovereign power, which gave rise to this complicated procedure, is now a thing of the past; at the present time the danger lies not in over-zealous prosecution, but in the escape of the guilty from conviction. The scheme of procedure is far too elaborate and complex; it greatly needs to be simplified and abbreviated.

The successive steps leading from the original charge to the final judgment afford the prisoner three distinct opportunities to escape prosecution. There are virtually three trials. First, upon the preliminary examination, all the evidence on both sides can be produced; the prisoner, aided by legal counsel and confronted with the witnesses against him, can cross-examine those witnesses and can produce all the counter-evidence at his command to establish his innocence. If he succeeds in convincing the committing magistrate that the charge has not been sustained, he obtains his immediate release and the prosecution ends; if, on the contrary, the magistrate is convinced that the prisoner is guilty, the proceeding has no corresponding finality for the prosecution. The prisoner is then committed for a second trial before the grand jury. Here again the testimony is reviewed, and further evidence can be adduced at the discretion of the grand jury; and here, as in the former trial, if the grand jury deem the charge unsustained, the prisoner gains his discharge, but, if the decision is adverse to the prisoner, he is committed for his third and final trial. In both the first trial before the committing magistrate and in the second trial before the grand jury a decision in favor of the prisoner is final (subject, in both cases, to a renewal of the prosecution by the district attorney); but a decision in favor of the prosecution has only the effect of granting a further trial.

It is difficult to understand why the forms of criminal procedure should differ so widely from the procedure in civil actions. A civil suit, at law or in equity, though it may involve many million dollars, is heard and decided, once for all, in a single trial. No civil case (except an action of ejectment and proceeding for probate of a will) can have a second trial, as of course. Why should a criminal case be subjected to so different a regimen? It would seem that, in the series of proceedings leading up to conviction, at least the second hearing, that before the grand jury, could well be eliminated. The intervention of the grand jury between the committing magistrate and the trial court serves no perceptible purpose that is either necessary or useful.

In practice, the chain of procedure is often abbreviated by cutting off the first link instead of dropping out the second one. The accusation of crime may be brought in the first instance, not before a committing magistrate but directly before the grand jury. But this practice gives rise to a positive and grave objection to the institution of the grand jury, as now constituted. When the original charge is laid before the committing magistrate, the accused person (as we have seen) is immediately summoned, he has the aid of legal counsel, he hears and cross-examines the witnesses against him, he has every opportunity to understand and to defeat the charge brought against him. The procedure before the grand jury may be widely different from this; its proceedings are secret, they may be conducted without the knowledge of the defendant and may result, upon strictly *ex parte* evidence, in an indictment charging the defendant with grave crime. Here are the possibilities of cruel injustice: groundless charges brought maliciously and supported by false testimony, a secret hearing and a final indictment, the first intimation of which comes to the innocent victim when he is thrown into prison with the certainty before him of a public trial. It all sounds like a happening from the middle ages, and yet it may possibly be the real experience of any resident of a state where the grand jury sits in secret with its present powers. No man (unless he be in hiding or otherwise inaccessible) ought to be subject to the public disgrace and brand of an actual indictment for crime, without having had opportunity to know what crime is laid to his charge, and by whom, and to assert his innocence. An indictment, in popular estimation, overthrows the presumption of innocence and creates a presumption of guilt; and when an innocent person is publicly indicted for crime, his reputation receives a stain which fades, but cannot be wholly effaced, by his subsequent trial and acquittal.

There are those who have urged the abolition of the grand jury as an outworn relic of medievalism. But there are times and occasions when the grand jury serves a most useful purpose in attacking public evils and in awakening the public conscience. Moreover, it sometimes enters upon investigations that must be conducted secretly to be effective. But its procedure in the investigation at first instance of a criminal charge should be radically altered and made to conform more closely to that now applicable to a committing magistrate. The person accused, if he is within reach, should be brought before the grand jury and allowed the fullest opportunity to refute the charge preferred against him. If he has absconded or cannot be found, the incriminating evidence should be received, and, if it justifies an indictment, an indictment should be found; but when the defendant returns or is brought again within the jurisdiction of the court, he should be produced before the grand jury then sitting, which should be invested with power to rehear the case, affording the defendant ample opportunity of exculpation, and with power upon such rehearing to either vacate or reaffirm the prior indictment or to find a new indictment. In this manner, every defendant would have a chance to establish his innocence before he could be brought to trial upon an indictment.

There are other features of the criminal procedure that are in sharp contrast with the practice in civil cases; and every such deviation from civil procedure secures an advantage to the defendant which in a civil suit would be regarded as repugnant to justice. In a criminal trial the defendant cannot be compelled to testify upon the facts in issue, and his refusal is held to create no presumption against him; in a civil action, a defendant who refused to testify on the ground that his evidence might aid the plaintiff's case would be apt to occasion some hilarity, ending in his commitment to prison for contempt of court.

In a criminal case, if the defendant's witnesses reside outside of the state, he is entitled to have their testimony taken on commission and admitted on the trial. The prosecution may join in such commission, and examine in support of the indictment other witnesses who happen to be within the state or country to which the commission is issued. But no right to the issuance of a commission is accorded to the prosecutor, who (with the exception just mentioned) is confined to the testimony of such witnesses only as are within the jurisdiction of the state and can be produced in person before the court. This rule gives a most unfair advantage to the defendant, whose witnesses are generally friendly to him and willing to appear in his behalf, while the witnesses for the state are often reluctant to testify and seek to evade the duty (and perhaps the danger) of appearing against the defendant. There is a provision in the Constitution of the United States, that in all criminal trials the accused shall have the right "to be confronted with the witnesses against him." This applies only to trials in the federal courts, but the same provision has been adopted in many of the states by constitutional or statutory enactment. "Confrontation" has been uniformly interpreted as meaning the personal attendance of the witnesses in the presence of the accused, but the requirement of such personal attendance extends only to the witnesses *against* the prisoner, not to those in his favor. The Common Law required the personal attendance of the witnesses against the defendant, but it also required the personal attendance of the defendant's witnesses as well. By the existing American system, the state may be deprived of the evidence of every witness who is beyond the reach of its territorial jurisdiction, while the prisoner has the unlimited power to secure by commission and to introduce in evidence, the testimony of absent witnesses from the ends of the earth—of witnesses who may, perhaps, have departed from the state for the express purpose of avoiding the necessity of attending in person at the trial and undergoing a searching cross-examination which might result in their immediate arrest on the charge of perjury or other crime. It may well be seriously questioned whether the existing system does in this regard serve the ends of justice or yield adequate protection to the state in the contest against crime.

A still more striking instance of partiality toward the prisoner appears in the procedure relating to appeals. For every error of law occurring during the entire course of the proceeding from the empanelling of the grand jury to the final conviction, for every erroneous ruling of the court upon the admission or rejection of evidence or upon the allowance or disallowance of challenges or upon the decision of any motion or demurrer, the defendant has an unlimited right of appeal. On the other hand, the right of the people to appeal is most rigidly restricted. From a judgment of acquittal there is absolutely no appeal in any case; though the acquittal was the immediate result of grave legal error committed by the judge in the rejection or admission of testimony, the state is powerless to have such error reviewed or corrected. Indeed, the only instance in which the state has any right to appeal from any decision or action of the trial córt favorable to the defendant, is where the court has sustained defendant's demurrer to the indictment. There are only two other cases in which the state is allowed the right of appeal at all; it can appeal from an order arresting a judgment of conviction and from a judgment reversing a judgment of conviction. Against this meagre allowance to the state of power to correct legal errors by appeal, the code, after giving to the defendant unlimited rights of exception and appeal at every step in the proceedings, contains this final provision, as if to emphasize the discrimination in his favor:

> The appellate court may order a new trial if it be satisfied that the verdict against the prisoner was against the weight of evidence or against law, or that justice requires a new trial, whether any exception shall have been taken or not in the court below.

But what if the verdict was *in favor* of the prisoner, but was against the weight of evidence or against law, and justice requires a new trial? The appellate court cannot then grant a new trial, because the code provides no means of bringing such a case before the appellate court. But take the solitary case in which the state is allowed to appeal from a judgment in favor of the prisoner; that is, a judgment sustaining his demurrer to the indictment. Suppose the appellate court is of the opinion that the demurrer ought to be sustained, but that the objection on which the demurrer was based might be avoided in a new indictment. In such a case, the code contains no section giving the appellate court power to direct the resubmission of the case to the grand jury.

The unrestricted right of appeal on the part of the prisoner given, and almost encouraged, by the codes has proved a very serious evil in this country. Successive appeals, devoid of merit, are taken, partly to gain time and partly in the hope of succeeding on some sheer technicality, which involve heavy expense to the state, yield encouragement to criminals, and scandalously delay the execution of justice. This evil has been intensified many-fold by the fact that such appeals have sometimes resulted in the discharge of the prisoner, where the appellate court has been controlled by its zeal to condemn legal errors, that really occurred in the course of the proceedings, rather than to show, by a broad view of the entire case, that such errors did not materially affect the final result. It is an axiom that the value of a penal system depends largely upon the certainty and the celerity with which crime is followed by conviction and execution of the sentence. The unlimited right of appeal given to the prisoner is opposed to this certainty and celerity An amended system seems quite practicable, by which an appeal should be allowed only upon a certificate by the judge who tried the case or a judge of a supreme court that there is reasonable doubt whether the result reached at the trial is not against law, or whether justice does not require a new trial. And there is no perceptible reason why, upon such a certificate, an appeal should not be allowed to the state as well as to the prisoner.

All criminal laws exist for the protection of the people. The life of the state, the safety of the individual and the very preservation of civilization itself are all conditioned upon the repression of crime. The enforcement of the criminal law is so vitally imperative that a criminal trial involves issues that are really momentous. It is not the fate of the individual prisoner only that is to be determined; the necessity that crime should be condemned, in the interest of the whole people, presents a paramount issue at stake in the trial. It is quite as important that the prisoner, if guilty, should receive condemnation, as it is that the prisoner, if innocent, should not suffer punishment. The common saying, that it is better that the guilty should be acquitted than that one innocent person should be condemned, embodies a theory that finds abundant expression in the codes of criminal procedure. The saying may be true, if the trial is regarded as affecting nothing but the individual destiny of the prisoner. But a criminal trial involves a much larger issue. The right of the people to protection against crime is quite as important as the right of the prisoner to a fair trial. Any system of criminal procedure that guards the right of the prisoner more sedulously than the right of the people, which secures to the prisoner facilities and advantages that it denies to the people, is a radically defective system.

Such a system diminishes public respect for law and emboldens crime. The difficulty in obtaining legal evidence of crime, with which the state is hampered, the legal technicalities and the right to secure testimony from absent witnesses, the rights of exception and appeal, all placed at the disposal of the prisoner and withheld from the state, the long delays and the uncertainty of the final result; these facts tend to create in the public mind a distrust of existing criminal procedure and cause it to be regarded as an ineffective and inadequate means of crushing crime. This distrust is the direct cause of the lynchings and the riotous outbreaks that are the disgrace, and almost the distinctive disgrace, of this country.

These express the popular contempt for a legal system that exhibits more zeal in protecting the prisoner than in protecting the public.

The ideal system of procedure is one that dispenses even-handed justice, that acts directly and simply, without cumbrous machinery, and that reaches results with certainty and celerity.

Before concluding this chapter, there remains a branch of criminal procedure of grave importance, regarding which the provisions of the code already cited are very meagre and inadequate; namely,

THE DEFENSE OF INSANITY

This defense assumes special importance because it is apt to be interposed, as the only possible defense, to crimes peculiarly atrocious. The very enormity of these crimes seems to indicate something inhuman and abnormal in the perpetrator that gives plausibility to the plea of insanity. In such case, as already stated, the New York Code of Criminal Procedure empowers the court to appoint a commission to report as to the sanity of the defendant when he committed the crime. If the commission reports that the defendant was insane at the time of the commission of the crime, the code is silent as to what action the court is to take with reference to the report or with reference to the defendant. It may be inferred, however, that in such case the execution of the commission takes the place of a trial; for the section which empowers the court to appoint the commission declares that the court may make such appointment "instead of proceeding with the trial of the indictment." The power to appoint is permissive and not mandatory, and as a matter of actual practice it is seldom used; ordinarily, the jury at the trial passes upon the insanity of the defendant as upon any other defense interposed. This is a serious wrong, because a jury drawn by lot from the common people is wholly incompetent to decide the issue intelligently. The question of sanity or insanity admits of no satisfactory solution except by scientific diagnosis. In many cases, the defendant stands near the border line between the two, where a correct judgment can be formed only by an experienced and highly trained alienist. The question is admitted to be one that must be decided by expert testimony, and so a number of so-called experts are produced as witnesses, those on the part of the prosecution asserting the sanity and those on the part of the defense asserting the insanity of the defendant. But the bewildered jury is probably more unable to decide intelligently between the experts than it is to decide the main issue of sanity or insanity without any expert testimony at all. The rudimentary principle in jury trials that the jury cannot pass upon questions of *law* is based on the fact that law is a science, but the question of sanity is not less scientific and is often as involved and difficult as any question of law.

This opens the whole difficult subject of expert testimony. Among the suggestions that have been made toward its solution, one that has been largely advocated calls for the selection and appointment of expert alienists as public officials who shall alone be called as expert witnesses upon the issue of sanity or insanity; but whether the suggestion can constitutionally be carried into effect demands careful consideration. There appears, however, no room for doubt that some method ought to be devised which shall take away from the common jury the function of determining the defendant's sanity or insanity and which shall commit the decision of that issue to a tribunal which is competent to treat it as a scientific question and to render a judgment that shall be final and conclusive.

A commission *de lunatico*, according to the prevailing practice, is composed of three commissioners (two of whom are usually a lawyer and a physician) appointed by the court and a sheriff's jury of not less than twelve nor more than twenty-four members. The same objection applies to this commission as to the ordinary trial-jury; the tribunal does not possess knowledge or experience to deal with an issue that lies in the domain of psychological and of physiological science and demands the education and practiced insight of the professional alienist.

The following plan is here proposed for meeting the plea of insanity. The first step should be a trial of the issue thus raised, to be had before the court and a special jury, the latter to consist of educated alienists only, who should be selected by a method analogous to that used to obtain a "struck jury." It is not necessary nor practicable that this jury should have twelve members; a much smaller number, perhaps five or even three, would be quite sufficient. This deviation from the traditional number of jurors (recommended for convenience) could not be made in those states the constitution of which requires a Common Law jury of twelve, without constitutional amendment. The constitutions of some of the states now provide for juries of eight, and even of four, members. The provision for jury trials contained in the United States Constitution requires a jury of twelve as at Common Law, but it applies to the federal courts only and places no restriction upon the power of a state to regulate the size of its own juries. The court and jury thus constituted, after examining the defendant and receiving such testimony bearing upon his sanity as might be offered by either party, should determine whether defendant was insane to a degree rendering him irresponsible for his acts at the time of committing the crime charged and also at the time of the trial before them. The judgment rendered should be final and conclusive, subject to an appeal upon errors of law if allowed by a judge of a court of general jurisdiction. The results arrived at by such a trial and the subsequent proceedings would classify themselves under four distinct headings.

1. If the defendant was insane when the crime was committed and is still insane, the judgment would forthwith commit him to an asylum. In case he should in the future become sane, he should not be released without a further trial, before a court similarly constituted, to determine whether his condition, mentally and morally, is such that his restoration to freedom would be consistent with "public peace and safety."

2. If the defendant was insane when the crime was committed but is now sane, the judgment would further determine whether his present condition is so entirely sane and normal that he can with safety to the public and himself be set at liberty; and if not, the judgment would forthwith commit him to a sanitarium or other suitable institution for treatment and observation until he could safely be discharged. In this as in the preceding case, the defendant would be forever exempt from a criminal prosecution for the crime in question.

3. If the defendant was sane when the crime was committed and is now sane, the judgment would direct that he be forthwith brought to trial before a criminal court and common jury, where the claim of insanity should be rigidly excluded.

4. If the defendant was sane when the crime was committed but is now insane, the judgment would forthwith commit him to an insane asylum where he should remain until he becomes sane; if he regains his sanity, he is then to be tried criminally with the same force and effect as if he had never been insane.

INDEX

INDEX

ADMIRALITY AND MARITIME JURISDICTION, 24

ANSWER TO INDICTMENT, 98

ANTI-TRUST LAW, 13, 30

APPEALS (IN CRIMINAL PROCEDURE), 103, 108

ARRAIGNMENT, 98

ARREST, 95

ARTICLES OF CONFEDERATION BETWEEN THE THIRTEEN ORIGINAL STATES, 2

ATONEMENT FOR CRIME, 61

ATTAINDER, 11

AVERAGE SENTENCES, 40

BAIL, 96

BAKER, F. M.: Trial for bigamy, 43

BERTILLON SYSTEM, 53

BIGAMY AND DIVORCE LAWS, 43

CAPITAL PUNISHMENT: United States penal code of 1909, 22

CHILDREN'S COURTS: Child labor and truancy laws, relation to, 84; Children's courts and probation officers (Eugene Smith), 75; Court of equity, 82; Denver juvenile court, communication with public schools, 85; Dependent and neglected children, jurisdiction over, 83; Exceptional qualifications required in judges, 83; Illinois juvenile court law, 78; Lindsey, B. B., rare personal qualities, 85; Prevention of crime by juvenile courts, 81; Separation from other courts, 84. See also *Juvenile Delinquents*

COMMON LAW OF ENGLAND: Accessories and principles, rule, 22; Age limit for capability of crime, 75; Criminal procedure, 104; Dealings with delinquent children, 77; Influence on federal and state penal codes, 3, 4, 16, 27; Interpretation of statutes, 33

COMPLEXITY OF CRIMINAL PROCEDURE, 105

CONSTITUTION OF THE UNITED STATES; adoption, 2

CONTINENTAL CONGRESS, 2

CRIME: Increase of, 56, 64; Prevention of—Prevention of crime by juvenile courts, 81

CRIMINAL INSANITY: Defence of insanity, 101, 111

CRIMINAL STATISTICS: Imperfect compilation in the United States, 55

DAVIS MURDER TRIAL, 28

DEFINITIONS OF CRIMES, 59

DENVER (COL.) JUVENILE COURTS, 85

DETECTION OF CRIMINALS, 53

DISCHARGED PRISONERS: Small percentage of reformations, 64

DISPOSITION OF CASE FOR TRIAL, 96

DISTRICT OF COLUMBIA: Cession of territory by Maryland, 15; Government, 12

DIVORCE AND BIGAMY LAWS, 43

DUAL SYSTEM OF GOVERNMENT IN THE UNITED STATES, 3, 6, 27

ENGLISH COLONIES IN NORTH AMERICA, 1

EVIDENCE: Rules of, 100

EXAMINATION (IN CRIMINAL PROCEDURE), 95

EXPERT TESTIMONY, 112

EXTRADITION BETWEEN STATES, 11, 54

FACTORS IN A TRUE ESTIMATE OF GUILT, 60

FARM WORK BY CONVICTS, 52

FASSETT LAW (PRISON LABOR), 49

FEDERAL COURTS, 14

117

FEDERAL CRIMINAL LAW, 14

FEDERAL GOVERNMENT AND THE SEVERAL STATES: Relations between, 1

FEDERAL PENAL CODE, 17, 18, 20

FINGER PRINT SYSTEM, 53

GRAND JURY: Composition and duties, 97; Objections to secret sessions, 106

GUILT: True estimate of, 60, 62

"HELD TO ANSWER" (IN CRIMINAL PROCEDURE), 95

IDENTIFICATION OF CRIMINALS, 53

ILLINOIS: Indeterminate sentence law, 73; Juvenile court law, 78

IMPEACHMENTS, 10

INCREASE OF CRIME, 56, 64

INDETERMINATE SENTENCE: Absolute indeterminate sentence not yet tested, 74; Capital crimes, non-applicability, 69; Constitutionality of laws, 73; Danger of premature adoption, 72; Definition, 67; Federal prisoners debarred, 23; Petty misdemeanors, 70; Recent origin, 71; Smith, Eugene, "The indeterminate sentence," 65

INDICTMENTS, 97, 98, 106

INEBRIETY: Treatment of, 70

INFORMATION (IN CRIMINAL PROCEDURE), 94

INJUSTICE OF MANY ASSUMPTIONS IN PENAL CODES, 59

INTER-STATE COMMERCE LAW, 13, 27, 35

ITALY: Controversy with the United States over New Orleans incident, 5

JAPANESE SUBJECTS IN SAN FRANCISCO, 9

JUDGMENT (IN CRIMINAL PROCEDURE), 102

JURY, 97, 101, 106

JUVENILE COURTS. See Children's Courts

JUVENILE DELINQUENTS: Age limit, 75, 80; Confinement of children in jails, 77; Medical treatment, 85; Moral sense, slow development of, 77. See also Children's Courts; Probation

LABOR: Competition with free labor, 46; Contract system—Abolition in New York, 48; Farm work, 52; Fassett law, 49; "Hard labor" in federal penal code, 22; Hostility of labor unions, 45; Lease system, 47. New York—Legislation, 47; Public account system, 48. Road-making, 52

LINDSEY, BEN B.: Exceptional qualities as judge of children's court, 85

LIVINGSTON, EDWARD: United States penal code, 21

MASSACHUSETTS: Probation laws, 87

MICHIGAN: Indeterminate sentence law, 73

NEAGLE MURDER TRIAL, 29

NEW ORLEANS (LA.): Murder of Italians by mob, 5

NEW YORK: Prison labor legislation, 47; Probation commissions, 92, 93

PARENTAL RESPONSIBILITY, 80, 82

PAROLE AND PROBATION: Distinction between, 88

PROBATION: Central board in cities, 92; Children's court and probation officers (Eugene Smith), 75; Expenditures for relief of probationers, 89; Massachusetts laws, 87; New York probation commissions, 92, 93. Officers—Appointment, 91; Civil service examinations, 91; Duties, 87; Qualifications, 89; Volunteer and salaried officers, 90. Parole and probation, distinction between, 90; Power of court to suspend sentence, 103; Suspension of sentence without supervision, 86

PROCEDURE IN CRIMINAL CASES, 94

PROCEEDINGS AFTER VERDICT AND BEFORE JUDGMENT, 102

PUBLIC PROTECTION: Rightful object of criminal law, 65

PUNISHMENT: Theories, 57, 65

PUNITIVE SYSTEM OF CRIMINAL LAW, 57

REFORMATION: Modern system of reformatory treatment, 66

RESPONSIBILITY: Parental responsibility, 80, 82

RETRIBUTIVE THEORY OF PUNISHMENT, 57, 65

ROAD-MAKING BY CONVICTS, 52

SAN FRANCISCO (CAL.): Treatment of Japanese subjects, 9

SENTENCE: Length of—Average sentences, 40; Unfair and unequal sentences, 63; Varying penalties in different states, 39

SMITH, EUGENE: "Criminal law in the United States", 1-113

STATE CRIMINAL LAW, 38

SUPREME COURT OF THE UNITED STATES, 15

TREASON, 11

TREATY OBLIGATIONS: Enforcement of, 5-10

TRIAL BY JURY, 11

TRIALS: Conduct of, 99

UNITED STATES CONSTITUTION: Adoption, etc., 2

UNITED STATES CRIMINAL LAW: Act of 1866, enactment and re-enactment, 19; Anti-Trust law, 30; Attainder, 11; Common law of England, influence of, 3, 4, 16, 22, 27, 33, 75, 104; Congress, powers of, 27; Counterfeiting foreign securities, 5; "Crimes Act" of 1790 and 1825, 17; Criminal law within federal jurisdiction, 14; Criminal law within the jurisdiction of the states, 38; Criminal statutes enacted by Congress, 4; Detection of criminals, 53; Divorce and bigamy, 43; Dual nature of government, 3, 6, 27; Extradition between states, 11, 54; Federal and state governments, relations between, 3, 12; Federal courts, 4; Federal penal codes, 17, 18, 20; General federal legislation, 26; Impeachments, 11; Inter-State Commerce law, 13, 27, 35. Jurisdiction —Admiralty and maritime, 24; Concurrent, of the nation and the states, 24, 28; Exclusive, of the nation, 15, 16; Federal jurisdiction in general, 10, 12. Livingston, Edward, penal code, 21; Local legislation, 15; Penal provisions in civil laws, 27; Punitive system of criminal law, 57; Smith, Eugene, "Criminal law in the United States," 1-113; State codes, wide differences, 38; Statistics, imperfect compilation, 55; Supreme Court, 15; Treason, 11; Treaty obligations, enforcement of, 5-10; Trial by jury, 11

UNITED STATES CRIMINAL PROCEDURE: Answer to indictment, 98; Appeals, 103, 108; Arraignment, 98; Common Law system, 104; Complexity of scheme, 105; Contrast with civil procedure, 107; Difficulty in securing convictions, 110; Disposition of case for trial, 96; Evidence, 100; Expert testimony, 112; Grand jury, 97, 106; Indictments, 87, 98, 106; Insanity as a defence, 101, 111; Judgment, 102; Jury, 97, 99, 101, 106; Partiality toward the prisoner, 107; Proceedings after verdict and before judgment, 102; Trials, conduct of, 99; Verdict, 101

UNITED STATES SUPREME COURT, 15

VERDICT (IN CRIMINAL PROCEDURE), 101